Evil and the Christian Faith

Evil
and the *Christian Faith*

by

NELS F. S. FERRÉ

Essay Index Reprint Series

BOOKS FOR LIBRARIES PRESS
A Division of Arno Press, Inc.
New York, New York

BJ1401
F4
1971

INTERNATIONAL STANDARD BOOK NUMBER:
0-8369-2393-6

LIBRARY OF CONGRESS CATALOG CARD NUMBER:
71-134075

To My Brothers

DR. GEORGE FERRÉ
REV. FOLKE FERRÉ
REV. C. GUSTAVE FERRÉ

Contents

viii   CONTENTS

Preface

Evil is always our central problem. Today we are almost overwhelmed by it. Wherever I lecture this is the problem on which people ask me to concentrate. The eager response keeps humbling me, causing me to search more deeply still. What can be more gratifying than to see people truly helped in their thinking, set free to believe, their lives lifted by a better-founded faith?

Evil has always been my central problem. This was so long before I met up with it in an intense personal encounter. It is precisely because the Christian faith solves the problem of evil with amazing adequacy that I have become so convinced a Christian. It solves evil in thought; it solves evil in life.

Kind critics have pointed out that nowhere in my writing have I dealt with the problem of evil. This has been true because I have wanted to approach the subject as fully as possible. This volume gives the very heart of my theology, the meaning of experience, history, and nature in relation to God's eternal purpose.

Naturally the formulation of the answer is not finished. Many new insights have come within the last two years, one or two of the most important within the last few months. Always we should grow. William F. Frazier in a devotional address this very morning pointed out that only the new growth of the vine bears fruit. The branches that did not grow the year before may bear leaves, help to sustain life, but never bear fruit. To be alive enough to bear fruit we must have growing edges. Yet whatever new formulations of the problem may come, the heart of my understanding and living is interpreted in this volume.

The structure of the book has a checkered history. Originally the whole of it was contained within the same manuscript that included *Faith and Reason*. Yet it seemed unwise to publish more than eighty thousand words in one book. Besides, *Faith and Reason* is a topic all its own, while evil is also too central a theme to be relegated to one section at the end of a lengthy work.

Thus *Faith and Reason* was published separately. I then wrote a new draft of *Evil and the Christian Faith*. For already I had decided to postpone to some future volume the section in the original manuscript on society! When this was ready, I asked to have it read by my close friend Edgar S. Brightman of Boston University and in part by my own beloved colleague, Paul S. Minear. They were severe critics.

At the suggestion of one of them I deleted a large section on the description of the most high of history. What I now do is simply to accept the most high as a given in history and test its adequacy against the problems we face—whether it gives the fullest possible explanation of our problems and the actual authority and motivation to solve them, whether it most fully and meaningfully explains all of life and gives power over all possible evil for all possible good.

The next stage was one of almost brutal condensation. The section on the Christian faith was a book in itself. It seemed, however, that, lest some material should appear to be repetitious to those who had read several of my previous books, it could be dispensed with.

Once I even considered not including any section on the Christian faith, simply referring any new reader to previous works. But that seemed troublesome and unfair to the reader. Finally I decided to include an appendix, on which I labored extra hard to give new light and elaborations important even for faithful readers.

A second appendix will refresh the memory of the readers of
Faith and Reason. It may also help new readers. Yet the first
volume is far too basic to be summarized. It is itself almost a
summary. This second volume as it now stands, however, is open
to any reader whose primary interest is the problem of evil.

As to future volumes, sufficient unto the book is the evil thereof.
I have still a large section left from the original manuscript on
the adequate interpretation of the Bible. This may precede the
projected volume on social problems. Out here on the ranch I
am learning to sit more loosely in the saddle. Our little schemes
often seem all-important, yet the Spirit cannot be thus forced for
a long future.

I am thankful to Professor Hocking for his last lecture on
the problem of evil in Metaphysics 9, which gave me the start
I needed.

It is a joy to dedicate the volume to my brothers, whose lives
of Christian service in the ministry and in medicine have been an
inspiration to me. My wife as always is at one with me in work as
well as in prayer. She is the most intimate sharer of my fellowship of inquiry. The whole family, in fact, give me hearty back-
ing and arrange their activities so that I may write. Day after
day the children pray with utter faith: "Give Daddy the right
words today."

I have never felt happier about a book. Not that it could not
be greatly improved; but I know that it has a much needed message at a most crucial time.

NELS F. S. FERRÉ

Sylvan Dale Ranch
Loveland, Colorado
August 7, 1946

Evil and the Christian Faith

CHAPTER I

Introduction

The most damaging evidence against our right to the full identification of what is most high and most real[1] is the fact of evil. There is no easy way out of this predicament. Either we must be able to suggest some lines of solution that have sufficient merit to call for conviction both intellectually and practically or else we have to admit that religion, as far as we can see, cannot constitute the whole-response which satisfies our highest thinking as well as the rest of our nature. Although explanation in thought is not central to right religion, it is nevertheless necessary to it. Strong religion is not a matter of trusting, after shutting one's eyes. It is rather trusting beyond the best that one can see with one's eyes open.

Mere academic speculation, of course, cannot be endured in days like these. We need living truth. The problem of evil is definitely no matter for mere part-thinking. Truth requires the whole man thinking. Those who can practice armchair philosophy on that hot spot must be impervious at their existential nerve endings. Sensitivity is rather the prerequisite for the kind of thinking that counts on this subject. *Detachment here is death to truth.* Evil is the central problem of religion. A whole-problem, involving the very center of life, cannot be solved except by whole-thinking. Whole-thinking presupposes whole-living, whole-

---

[1] As seen in *Faith and Reason*.

living with the problem, including much long and strenuous thought on the subject.

Insofar as we all succeed or fail here we can talk with or without legitimate conviction about solving the problem of evil. Our whole understanding of truth, as analyzed in *Faith and Reason*, requires this basic approach. Theology depends upon depth-devotion in order to combine both critically and creatively sound thinking.

Yet as a matter of fact, when all is said and done the actual solution of the problem of evil must by the nature of things be beyond our best seeing, for it is centrally in the realm of the dynamic creativity and the divine redemption experienced in the midst of personal and social evil, experience alone affording the insight and adding the grace of clinching conviction. The only full solution of evil is the overcoming of it. Those who do overcome, to whatever degree, that far know the more intimately. This is the reason for the otherwise astounding fact that many who have struggled most deeply with the problem of evil in their own lives and thought are least oppressed by it, provided they have struggled, of course, with faith in, and with the help of, a power immeasurably better than and beyond their own.

To begin with, we warn against starting with *partial perspectives* as substitutes for the fullest perspective possible on the subject. A partial perspective is one that cannot constitute the criterion of the full truth and therefore cannot adequately define the problem. If we start with such perspectives it is only to show why they are partial. We must also warn against *mixed perspectives*. Intellectually they are more dangerous and destructive than mixed drinks. They engender confusion and spiritual nausea beyond easy recovery. Many start, for instance, with a perfect God of redemptive love as a standard. Then alongside Him they put up as another ultimate the standard of perfect pleasure. This world shows that they do not go together. Therefore God is limited. Thus they that far reason themselves spiritually under the table. They have two ultimate standards.

If, however, pleasure cannot constitute the ultimate principle of explanation, the full truth of the ultimate, it cannot be set alongside God as Agape, the kind of love that Jesus was and taught, as another absolute requirement on reality. If pleasure can constitute such an ultimate principle, then God is, of course, proved by this world not to be fully good, wise, or able. In either case we must choose one perspective or the other and subordinate the lesser to the greater. One perspective alone is ultimate. Our Christian perspective is God as Agape.[2] We must, therefore, proceed to ascertain whether or not this world squares confirmingly with that ultimate principle of explanation. The full truth alone can as fully as possible satisfy the mind and meet the demands of the facts.

If no one ultimate perspective can be found, we must, of course, readily acknowledge our conclusion. Dualism and pluralism are available choices. But we must be careful to reduce our fractions as far as possible. Often we fail to get to the basic solution because we cannot see through all the hidden relations of the factors involved. Our world of experience is too much of a universe to discard that depth-notion without adequate trial. We are offering what seems to us ever more compellingly a central and all-inclusive ultimate perspective. That being so, we have, to begin with, a right to warn against partial and mixed perspectives of truth.

[2] The reader who is not thoroughly acquainted with this interpretation of Christianity should consult Appendix A. Particularly important is the section on definitions.

CHAPTER II

The Level of Historic Fact

By the nature of the case we cannot find a solution of the problem of evil on the level of mere fact. By "fact" we mean a disjunct, concrete event in our history. We have already found in *Faith and Reason* that the facts of the here and now cannot constitute an adequate content for our existential ultimate,[1] cannot serve as an adequate criterion of the full truth. When we look at fact from the viewpoint of the problem of evil, however, we find the following further corroboration. If facts were truly what they are here and now, and nothing more, all that we could know is that there are good and evil, and that the relation between them is a baffling mystery. We have, however, seen right along in our analysis of method that all adequate explanation must be related to the whole. This relation, too, is not only organic but growing beyond its own immediate organic context. Our whole history is itself related to a Whole by means of which it is being transformed beyond the requirements of its own intrinsic capacities and nature. Present fact is thus capable of being changed not only because it is more than itself co-ordinately, that is, in its present outreach and in its present dependence on the process as a whole, and not only because it is more than itself genetically, more, that is, than the total accumulations of its pasts, but also because it is more than itself by virtue of what it can become, and is in fact condi-

[1] Cf. pp. 149 ff.

4

tioned and controlled to become, by its being related to One who is indescribably more than our process and who means and wills immeasurably more with and for it, having given it, in the first place, the urge to become, the power to become, and the stuff with which to become. We know that we are dealing primarily, not with a world of lastingly stubborn fact, but with a world that is more fluid than fixed.

To attempt, therefore, to solve the problem of evil on the level of fact, or simply to leave it there, is to make a false start. Facts are not mere facts. They are more than they seem. They are no isolated bits of eternal stuff. They are energy in change. Facts are made and constantly in the making. They are made and remade. They depend on function. Facts depend on their relation to the whole, to their place in the scheme of things at the time of that particular function. They depend on the Supreme in—but far more, beyond—our history, who acts, changes things, makes things different, new.

Even personal facts cannot stand still. They, too, must change with time. Though in eternity fact and function may be of equal importance, in our world of process function is far more important than fact, the verb than the noun, the direction of the process than the present point of attainment. As Roger Hazelton keeps hammering home: "We are more approaching than arriving; we are more anticipating than attaining." We live more by hoping than by having. Facts are mostly forms of function, in this world of ours, or functions in form. All things are in the making and for the making. The creative person always becomes more than he is; his reach goes far beyond his grasp; his heart is ahead of his feet. The more positively creative he is, moreover, the more he is characterized by the pointing of his life beyond the process as a whole to the farthest reach of it, to its Purpose, to its deepest meaning.

And no fact is merely a separate function, be it physical or personal. Every fact is what it is only within and because of these relations, these larger functions, these more inclusive prehensions.[2] It is what it is, even now, because of its relation to the whole which is not only its presupposed background but its presupposed bearer. These relations which make each fact more than it is as a mere fact are not static, primarily, or structural, but they are rather predominantly dynamic, functional, acting. The whole matters to its dynamic part. The wave of the ocean is different from the wave of the puddle even though the wind is equally strong in either instance. The smallest fact in our process is different because the ocean of being is far vaster than our present history. Its full meaning depends on the character of the fullest reality of which it is organically a part.

Facts, again, depend on time. We cannot freeze process and catch fact. The fact which we think we catch is an abstraction. The fact would not be what it is apart from the functioning of time. Perhaps we had better say that fact would not be fact at all without time, for in our history time is an essential aspect of process. Our facts are facts of process and as such are forms of functions. All in process acts and interacts. What is in process is what it is because it interacts. Interaction is never at an instant. Interaction is an event. It has duration. It is a dynamic occurrence which would not be what it is apart from the functioning of energy in time according to pattern.

Mere fact at an instant is a fiction of the intelligence. Mere fact is a false freeze. At a moment there is no reality of process and all the reality that we know is that of our process and through our process. Our knowledge is through and through dynamic. The real moves, changes, becomes. Even the ultimate must be existentially dynamic rather than speculatively static. Speculation need not arrive at the static, of course, but it is ever tempted to do so. When what is fact is made the standard of the ultimate, at least to the point where the ultimate is declared

---

[2] A prehension is Whitehead's more dynamic term for relation, consistent with organismic rather than substance philosophy.

polluted by the fact, the speculative intellect has frozen the process, judging it prematurely, rather than let it eventuate in its proper highest dynamic activity, its own proper reality.

In our process what was, is ever becoming what will be, via what is. The wasness of the was is different from the isness of the was. That means that the fact itself has been changed. The fact as mere fact was, but is no more. As it now is, it was not. It is now a part of a new fact and will be still different as the isness of the fact becomes an unreal wasness, and is, rather, a different isness within a new fact, functioning within it, both conditioning it and being itself changed by it. All creativity is dynamic change. All growth is process in alteration. We keep living all the while the place where we live is constantly being repaired and remodeled. Process never stops completely, as we know it, for repairs. All facts of process are being changed and changing.

What we know is energy according to patterns changing dynamically into ever new and different patterns. Sometimes there is much sameness or similarity of pattern. Sometimes the change is abruptly different. Nature is not mere repetition but dynamic change according to new formations within generally established forms of flux. History is the coming of the new conditioned by the past and broadly repeating past patterns yet withal constantly varying them. Facts are functions dynamically dependent upon their own past; upon the past of their most relevant environment; upon the past of the whole of nature or actuality; upon their own present decision; upon their present relations and the decisions of the facts to which they are most dependably related; upon the nature of their relations, beyond that, to future facts; upon functions pointing to ever new changes according to inner drives and organic functions within the whole of actuality, prompted by a whole which is not yet actual, itself dependent upon the nature of Him who supremely acts.

Facts are thus what was, the way it is modified by what is, for the sake of what shall be. Only the ultimate primarily combines equally all these aspects of process. Within process fact is primarily understood in terms of becoming. Obviously evil can never be viewed truly and significantly from the perspective of mere fact. Evil is never a mere fact. Nothing in history, even, is *mere* fact. Evil is always a part of, or an aspect of, some becoming. It is always directly or indirectly a thwarting or perverting of some becoming. It is ever a misdirection of function causing traffic snarls for more than itself because of the relatedness within process. Evil is ever an aspect of becoming more than of being.

All the evil that we know is within process and is therefore to be seen as false function. Positive function is basic. Creative becoming is the drive of process. False function in a world of constant becoming is never a final fact. The fact is never mere fact, but is ever to be judged for its worth and meaning in terms of that which truly functions and the way the function is truly heading. That is no denial of the presence of evil in process. Its being in process, however, is no final indication of the worth and truth of the Purpose of process that must be judged by the result and whether the end is better because of its having been there, or at least because of the kind of conditions which produced it having been there.

Thus evil can never be judged from the perspective of facts that merely are. Evil never is a mere fact. There is no totally evil fact. There is no single, unrelated, permanently satanic fact. We know of no static structure permanently contradicting the good. The evil that we know is adjectival. It is a minor, never a major, premise; a subordinate, never a co-ordinate, clause. For every evil that we know there is some greater good of which it is the evil. We do not even know a person who is totally evil and permanently frozen so. Such a description is a denial of the nature of positive process. What goes on goes on because of being, not non-being; power, not lack of it. What goes on, goes on often in contradiction to itself, negating itself, but we know of no permanent or final negation.

Evil, which we are soon to define, is frustration of being rather than the definition of it. From the perspective of the most high, from the point of view of the truth that alone can explain our being and beginning, process is by now just pushing significantly ahead. Truth based on the deepest and fullest implications of process as a whole and on our living response to it denies the presence of mere fact and the adequacy of any criterion of truth which is based on mere fact. Even the mere description of process shows us that all is in change insofar as it occurs within the limits of our process below the level of the most high, which can be explained by nothing less than itself and yet explains most adequately all else. Evil must thus be seen to a great extent in the light of becoming as that becoming illuminates the channels of that which has become. Yet the most important perspective is the point where process has become full, the point of perfection toward which the process as a whole, in terms of its fullest interpretation, even now *points*, though obscurely and without full rational confirmation.

In that light mere fact becomes much more than itself and, indeed, greatly different from itself. Present facts must be seen in the light of their relations, past, present, and future, within process and beyond it. Facts must be primarily related, however, to their future relations, unpredictable in detail by anyone because of the presence within process of real freedom, yet foreseeable in general because of God's sovereign conditioning and control of history. They must be seen basically in terms of the reflexive superspective.[3] This is the function of truth. This is the necessary work of the dynamic synthesis of faith and reason without which truth simply cannot be had.

Mere fact decides nothing about the nature of the ultimate. It only indicates what is now actual. Mere fact cannot explain. It cannot, therefore, judge in terms of totality of meanings. What is now actual has neither reality nor meaning, in any ultimate

[3] Cf. *Faith and Reason*, p. 150 f.

sense, apart from the past of process, its total present being, and above all the pointing of process which indicates its true nature and reality. The truth of a fact, as a whole, must be understood in terms of its basic relationships. The truth can be seen only in the why of the now in the light of the total, final meaning of the now itself. The fact that there is evil now, from our point of view, has no verdict in itself over the goodness, wisdom, or power, of God. That the means of effecting the fellowship are not now, not yet, perfected ends does not by itself mean that God is no greater than or as evil as the means.

What matters is, rather, whether evil has a rightful and needful function in the nature of process the way that process is pointing. Present evil must be judged not by the now but by the then, by its total function in process with regard to the final, full purpose for its being, or its being possible. The means must be judged by whether or not they are appropriate to and necessary for the effecting of the ends for which they are the means. If they are good, as seen dynamically by the full synthesis of faith and reason, evil is still actually evil but in the service of the good. Evil is then the fact that the ends are not yet attained, which is the reason for our experience of evil, since by our needs we are made for the ends, but being made in terms of our means.

The ultimate evil would then be that all be not ends; that there be existences which require means; that there be growth; that there be freedom; that there be finitude. Evil is then a speculative category. Existentially we have, rather, to start with our experience which life declares to be good particularly as it becomes better, approaches the ends by the means. If we were further along in the existential approach we could say that evil is due to the fact that we refuse to accept the good which God offers and that therefore the environment must also remain appropriate to our refusal, groaning in travail while awaiting the revealing of the sons of God.[4] Our basic experience of evil lies here. It is existen-

[4] Cf. Romans 8:19-22.

tially our lot, individually and socially, in inseparable intertwining. Yet the existential decision that solves evil actually cannot be used as a substitute for the explanation of evil in the relation of Purpose to process.

Fleeting evil facts may, within the perspective of the compossible, that is, from the point of view of those things which are possible together, defined in terms of the highest living meaning, in terms of God's act and meaning, be consistently contributory to the truest function of the fullest, eternal Purpose. Such facts may be the necessary functioning in the realization of God's true good. Only the nature of the Purpose and the fact whether or not the function of evil is needful intrinsically to the full realization of that Purpose, according to its nature, through a total process of our kind, can settle whether the full identification of the most high and the most real is justified by what we see. Any other level of interpretation is too low to meet the full demands of truth.

The real question is, thus, not whether or not evil is a true fact in process according to our experience, but whether or not it is intrinsically and justifiably instrumental in the Purpose of process. If so, we can distinguish between the temporary evil in process which has a necessary purpose for our highest eventual good, and is thus part of God's goodness toward us, and the evil which would be permanently part of reality because, as far as we can see, it has no merely temporary, formative, essential function in process. Either evil has no essential relation to the effecting of the good as a total end, being unnecessary even temporarily whether in kind or quantity or permanently obstructing the realization of the good as a total end, or else it has a permanent meaning as a necessary means to the realization of the total good as a permanent end. Even if we should find no full solution, even suggestively, to certain aspects of the problem, the burden of proof would still be on our ignorance rather than on the true light which we do see and rather than on the existentially best way, in which, in order to be most adequate in life and thought, we must walk.

We should have to say, however, that we cannot see how right religion can be a wholly legitimate whole-response. It would not only lack the affirmations of whole-reason but would also have to contend with negative, even if not positively contradictory, evidence. Faith would not be fully legitimate as truth because it would be contrary to certain finally recalcitrant facts. Our walking in the best way would then have to be with a divided mind and an anguished soul. Right whole-response cannot be lulled by its very nature into insincere rationalizations, however ingenious.

Not until we come to view evil on the fullest level of truth, however, can we begin to get an adequate answer to this question. Truth itself must first be allowed to speak. The context of truth that can best explain the becoming of our process must be allowed to show us whether or not it also has constraining answers regarding the ends of process and the meaning of evil in the light of those ends. That is truth, and only that, which best explains the beginning of process, its becoming, our practical problems, individually and socially, and finally which suggests most persuasively where our process is going, and how evil fits in from beginning to end, not theoretically alone, but existentially, including the best knowledge, as far as our own lives are concerned.

Unamuno has a right to insist that we deal directly with *The Tragic Sense of Life*. Had he only seen that reason can be in the service of life and that theodicy can and must be existential, if it is to be adequately explanatory! As a matter of fact, when it is compelling, it is existential to the very marrow of "the man of flesh and bone," whether the existential then be the desperate cry of the frustrated will to live or the calm peace of the fulfilled will to live, fulfilled already with a vision ánd power beyond physical death.

Before leaving this first level, the level of fact, we do not, we cannot, we must not, we do not want to deny the fact of evil.

Evil is an actual occurrence. Even if evil is an illusion, an "error of mortal mind," it is still an evil fact. It is still real to experience. If it is only a nightmare, this nightmare is an evil fact. Evil is a fact. A fact is an instance of actual experience or of true occurrence, whatever be its nature. We feel bad whether or not it be good in the end that we did feel bad. A Christian Scientist shoemaker once told the writer that when he hammered his finger by mistake he prayed God for the truth of the situation *until the finger stopped aching.* To call evil an illusion, negative, privative, a deficiency, non-being, or what not still leaves the problem on the level of fact exactly where it was before. It is still there both to be overcome in experience and to be more fully explained as to its actuality.

Let us summarize the brunt of our discussion of this level most simply: On the level of fact as such there can be no full solution of the problem of evil. Only the complete realization of the good at the end of our process can give us that, and then only if evil is a necessary condition within the intrinsic compossibles of Purpose as exemplified partially, but ascertainably, within process. A full solution requires, therefore, a view of the relation between Reality and process which absorbs as necessary to the highest final good the kind of conditions which involve evil. The full solution can accordingly be afforded only in terms of the reflexive superspective, the necessary synthesis of faith and knowledge required by the full nature of dynamic truth within the stages of process.

Our concern now, on the level of fact, is to point out that in an organic universe, characterized by continual change, where no facts are mere facts but mostly points of transition toward the fullness of Purpose, there can be, to use Royce's phrase, no "hell of the irrevocable." Every past is redeemable in its inmost reality inasmuch as it persists within each present, modifying it and being modified by it. If facts were *mere* facts there could never be any solution at all adequate. Then the past as past would have eternal meaning. God, at least, would have to remember it, but God is ever the God of a real present, including the living past, never the God of a dead past.

As it is, the past, *as past*, is unreal and without significance except as it persists in the present objectively and/or subjectively. The past is continually being reconstructed and, when canceled out, forgotten. When God forgives sins, He *automatically* also forgets, throws them behind His back, because they are no more. God never forgives, therefore, unless we also forgive all who owe us. His forgiveness otherwise would be the ineffective and unreal cancellation of the guilt. When there is full forgiveness all around, however, the consequences of guilt are also eventually canceled in nature.

Time is literally perishing, the content of time continually vanishing away. The level of fact, therefore, does not have to be, and cannot be, our perspective in attempting to throw light on the question of evil. This level is refused by the very nature of process itself, by the content of our best knowledge. The fact that evil *is* constitutes no final indication of the nature of Reality. The fact of evil must be interpreted for its full meaning and judged for its final reality in the light of our fullest truth.

CHAPTER III

The Aesthetic Level

The first level of approach was that of mere fact. The second is the aesthetic level. This is the level of partial solution by means of aesthetic contrast. The spectator who sees the whole picture can see the function of evil, it is claimed, why it is needed for the sake of the whole. This is an agelong approach to our problem, and it does give us, we readily admit, at least a partial solution. The full solution, nevertheless, is far from reached. The Stoic and his successors throughout the ages may talk about the perfect symphony which needs all the parts, even the atonalities. No participant in the playing, they say, can hear the full harmony. Those who play hear too much of their own little part, which is without full meaning by itself. Only the hearer of the full harmony can judge the beauty of the symphony as a whole. Only God, or Reason, they say, can understand and appreciate the whole, which requires the parts that by themselves, particularly to those who play them, may seem evil.

The skeptical philosophers have already given the right answer to this rationalization: It makes a great deal of difference whether you are the Whole hearing the symphony or whether you are one of the parts which must hear and bear the cacophonies. The parts that suffer have a right to deny, if this condition is permanent and to no adequate end, that the symphony is good. If God calls it perfectly good it merely reflects on His nature. What right does the Whole have to enjoy Himself at the expense of the parts? What God calls good is not good for us in any full sense until we, too, know and experience it as good. Calvin's explanation of hell to the effect that the infinite needs infinite representation has much in common with this level of interpretation, including the same disregard both for the nature of the Whole and for the experience of the unfortunate individuals within it. It is not enough to stress God's sovereignty; we must also stress the right kind of sovereignty.

The tourist may think the slums of a foreign city "fascinating." To go through them, however, is different from living in them. Tortures and hangings may be called "thrilling" by sadists, but hardly by the victims. The atomic bomb may fill us with a cosmic thrill—if it is confined to Buck Rogers, or at least is not near us. A burning house may be "a wonderful sight" to the onlookers, while those trapped inside may feel quite otherwise about it. In this process of ours we deal with life, not with mere paintings; with participants, not only with spectators; with hearts that ache and break and not only with poundings on a piano. We deal, in fact, with our own lives. We are the victims, those trapped. The aesthetic level does give a partial solution, a vicarious satisfaction, a spectator's thrill—but it definitely fails to give us a full solution for each and all.

What kind of aesthetic satisfaction the one who views the scene gets also depends upon what kind of person he is. Someone exclaims over the thrill he had in seeing a certain hotel burn down. But for the mother whose child was left in the burning building there was little sense of aesthetic satisfaction. When the hurricane stirred us with a sense of awe and majesty, the feeling was changed for the man whose son was pinned under a tree.

The saints in heaven, according to some theologians, are supposed to be reminded occasionally of their celestial felicity by looking down at the sinners in hell. But we suspect that neither the

writers who wrote this nor their saints were fully candidates for
the true beatitude! According to some theologians, lacking sensitivity and pathos, God's glory is supposed to find infinite representation by having even hell within His dynasty. We suspect,
however, that both such theologians and their Gods need mission-
aries to tell them of Christ's compassion. With us human beings,
unfortunately, is sadism, the joy of destroying, invidious delight
in others' suffering and loss. Not only does the aesthetic satisfaction solve evil only partially but much of the solution is itself
mixed, arising out of mixed, and not altogether satisfying, motives.

The aesthetic level unites the good and the bad into a present
whole of vivid contrast. Time is therefore ruled out as the main
factor in the solution. Even the drama lives by present suspense.
The point is the suspense more than the solution. To take away
the former is to spoil the drama. The end must not be fully revealed. There must be concealment. He who reads the novel or the
play by reading the last few pages first, forsakes art in order to
find refuge in religion. He will not read unless the book has a
"happy ending." He demands "anticipated attainment." The
aesthetic judgment is mainly, as Ralph Barton Perry has observed,
a judgment of perpetuation. The religious judgment, however, is
basically a revolutionary judgment with regard to the present.
This is one reason why religious literature is difficult except in
terms of devotion or worship. These are the native languages of
religion. A religious fiction is nearly impossible. Either it is
moralistic, demanding change, and not good aesthetics, or it deals
with the depths of experience dramatically but without full demand for the fastest possible elimination of the evil in the situation. In that case it is poor religion.

Music, too, may move and depend upon solutions; but the
movement, the music itself, the present contrast, is what is enjoyed, not its ending. It is not better that it be all over. The
music is not a means primarily to the reaching of ends. Much of
the aesthetic characterizes life, giving it present enjoyment and

zest. Yet as far as the problem of evil goes, the whole case of religion rests on evil's being over, its being done away. The process must be a means, at most only a necessary stage. Whatever good it contains must be as nothing in comparison to the good that will be revealed.

If eternity is treated spatially, moreover, as the full stretch of process or processes, with time, in the sense of our process, organically related to it as an integral part of it, there must be evil in eternity as well as in time. Else we use weasel words and evasive symbols. The best that we can then arrive at is Whitehead's continually frustrated God, the peace of the poet who suffers with his creations, the tragic sufferer who understands. Such a solution is more truthful and, to many, more comforting than the mental evasions which make the sufferings of the part disappear within the satisfactions of the aesthetic whole. Yet no full explanation of process itself can be had in terms of extension. Eternity and time cannot be treated as primarily congruent spaces. Transcendence and immanence cannot mean qualitatively the same thing; God inhabits eternity; man, time. The whole, if God be truly the God who can solve the problem of evil, is not merely the full circle, eternity, which contains all finite circles, our finite histories. God is not the whole, but rather He creates, sustains, rules, and redeems all that is other than Himself. God and His realm must be both carefully kept apart—in nature—and also carefully kept together—in His care and control—according to the demands of our existential ultimate. If our terms and thoughts are allowed to stay on the aesthetic level, and particularly if we use the spatial language of the spectator, we shall surely find no solution that can satisfy our most critical and creative whole-thinking. Serial thinking based on the analogy of natural causation and uninterrupted continuity is, in any case, a form of extensive thinking that precludes the satisfactory solution of our problem.

We have seen that we can solve the problem of evil neither on the level of fact nor on the level of the aesthetic satisfaction of the Whole. The only level that will do is the level of truth where by faith and reason the most high is also fully the most real. Yet we are in the predicament that the truth which we have found not only must illumine our subject but must even now to some extent be tested by its capacity to illumine it. We must show that the content of right religion better answers the problem of evil than the two previous levels. The reflexive superspective with which we work is God in Christ as the embodiment in history of the divine Agape. He is the "clarified anticipation" of what we are to become and therefore even now, although not actually yet, essentially are.

CHAPTER IV

The Personal-Spiritual Level

Why do we believe that this third level, the personal-spiritual, will illuminate as fully as possible the problem of evil? In the first place, precisely because it is *personal*. No historic fact, it is true, is ever a mere fact. Yet persons are additionally the kind of facts where meanings can be appropriated by depth-memory. Experience, therefore, can be transmuted in such a way that it is enriched by past failure and difficulty, even by perversity and rebellion. Where sin abounded grace can the more abound.[1] Physical facts, to be sure, also change and thus even nature can be restored. Since fact is nowhere in history or nature mere fact, nature can also be redeemed. Since, moreover, time is not real, since the past has no reality as such, the solution of evil in natural process is possible. Yet, even so, such evil in nature would be unnecessary, as far as we can see, and therefore would definitely reflect on Reality, if it were not for the necessary part which nature plays in the perfecting of process. Nature does not learn. Man learns by means of nature. More of this shortly. Only because there is a personal level, however, where experience can appropriate, make use of, the kind of environment which we know, can we see any solution to the problem why there should have been any evil necessary in the first place to the perfecting of process. As we presently shall pursue the theme of the reason for evil in process

[1] Cf. Romans 5:20.

through several aspects of process, it will become increasingly clear that it is only on the personal level that our problem can approach a satisfactory solution.

In the second place, the personal-spiritual level rejects at the outset all claims that there is any answer to the problem of evil which proceeds from the hedonistic premise. That premise makes pleasure the supreme good. Any world that ever contains suffering must, therefore, *ipso facto* be bad according to the amount of suffering it contains. If we start with this superficial standard of what a perfect world must be like, there naturally is no solution to our problem. We know that there is suffering. It is no use to resort to ingenious rationalizations. Problems must be met squarely and honestly if they are to be satisfactorily solved. What right do we have, however, to start with a vacation-at-the-beach philosophy of life? Why is the pleasure of the eternal picnic our highest standard of perfection ?

Are the deepest and best things that we have known bought without the price of difficulty? Are they not rather sometimes bought even at the price of suffering and sorrow? Are those who have never suffered at all our highest examples of excellence? Deep in its heart does the world declare that those are the best who have always had a soft, sheltered life of unbroken pleasure? We must start in whole-thinking, not in speculation; in actual life, not in daydreaming. Christian faith makes the Cross of Christ, with all that symbolizes and stands for, the central means for the effecting of the best. The fellowship of grace, the fellowship of mutual understanding, the fellowship of common tasks, the fellowship of forgiveness, the fellowship of the branches in the common Vine, of common care and concern for one and all because one is the Father of us all—that highest level of fellowship which can alone satisfy our lives at their depths is not created by any fiat, that cannot be made by any say-so. It is too slow and too deep in becoming, too precious in its actuality, too costly in its make up. When we accept the superspective which most fully finds us at

our deepest we start to solve the problem of evil not with our right
to total pleasure but with the costliness of redemptive love.

We must start with truth. Pleasure cannot satisfy the demands
of truth. Pleasure, that is, cannot explain the totality of our
process. Since there is much that is not pleasant it cannot, for
instance, constitute the highest principle of inclusiveness. It has,
furthermore, no adequate principle of concretion or of actualization. It cannot, again, for example, account for the novel emerg-
ences like consciousness and redemptive love, which often thwart,
interrupt, or even sacrifice pleasure to duty, or, higher, to responsible concern. Pleasure, therefore, cannot constitute the content of
our existential ultimate: that which cannot explain our being and
becoming most suggestively cannot ever qualify as the standard
of ultimate truth. Pleasure must not, therefore, be raised up as an
ultimate standard to test whether or not the most high is also
fully the most real. Pleasure, not being the standard of the full
truth, cannot even adequately define evil as its direct opposite.

Much trouble comes from our defining evil from a partial perspective. Partial perspectives have only partial power and partial
rights to define partial aspects of truth. Evil must be centrally
defined in terms of our highest known truth, that which best
explains the becoming of process and best answers the questions
addressed to our present situation by our whole-thinking. In line
with our basic definition of truth, consequently, *evil is that which
thwarts God's effecting of the universal Christian fellowship.*
This definition, however, is more existential than explanatory. It
is an explanation in terms of the now rather than of the now in the
light of the then. That which thwarts the effecting of the fellowship now may in the end help the most to effect it. That it be
possible is then intrinsic to the nature of process and not evil as a
means in the light of eternity. Man's freedom, for instance, thwarts
God's effecting the fellowship by man's insistence on being himself. Yet this thwarting of the fellowship by man's freedom now,
as we shall see shortly, may be the very core of God's method of

effecting the fellowship in depth, power, and lasting reality. From this point of view, suffering as a means may be a far greater good in many instances than pleasure. The hand of God which hurts us may in the end be better for us than the hand which openly helps us. Whether or not God is infinite, in any case, cannot be judged from the point of view of pleasure as the determining perspective. This is a mixing of perspectives fatal to true thinking.

Nor in a world containing at the same time freedom and vicarious living, and that on both the vertical and the horizontal levels, can individual cases be judged as such. Fact is never mere fact. There can only be legitimate general judgments. *That* evil will or choice, *that* bit, or life, of suffering, cannot be isolated from the totality of process in the light of which alone it has its full meaning, reality, and goal. The only valid question is, rather, if the truth of the end is big enough to include completely within the general solution an unstinted regard and concern for every individual life.[2] The basic question is whether suffering as such is evil as a means as well as an end, or if it is consistent with, and necessary to, the effecting of the highest ends of process.

Existentially speaking, furthermore, the hedonistic premise does not start with the highest that we know. We have all experienced pleasure. It is as nothing, we know, on the physical level in comparison to the spiritual. We have also experienced social approval and success. It is, to be sure, fun, exciting, and warming, but in itself it is hollow. We are perhaps but more lonely than before, in the depths of our being. The more pleasure from success that we have, the more wretched it seems in comparison to the depths of satisfaction which our souls seek. We have also experienced the pain of sacrifice, the pain of failure, and found through them, surprisingly, a power and a joy of spirit which is far beyond mere positive physical or social pleasure. We have

---

[2] The full efficacy and distribution of what we call evil cannot, naturally, *by the nature of the case*, be conclusively judged in terms of our flash of existence or peephole of vision.

experienced the spiritual victory over suffering which veritably opens new dimensions to life. We have found new levels of life in doing without in order to help the least brother, in counting others better than ourselves, and in commending our lives to God whether for pleasure or for pain, for success or for failure, for suffering or for well-being.

What we can say truthfully from experience is that pleasure as pleasure pales in comparison to the depths and wealth of life which flows from the power of the Cross of One who counted not the cost too great that he might do the will of God. "But the natural man receiveth not the things of the Spirit of God; for they are foolishness unto him: neither can he know *them*, because they are spiritually discerned. But he that is spiritual judgeth all things, yet he himself is judged of no man."[3] The natural man dreads suffering. He wants his world to be all pleasure. He dreads death. Yet the natural man finds no deep and lasting satisfaction for he goes plumb contrary to truth. Selfishness, especially the demand for a constant, positive satisfaction of our will to live for ourselves, cannot ever be satisfied. To start, therefore, with the law of the natural man and to judge the most high by it is to start wrong end to.

Our demand for perfect pleasure, moreover, may deep down in our lives be a desire to escape this actual world with its cross of responsibility before both God and man. We may call God finite and religion unreasonable in view of the kind of world in which we live simply because we do not ourselves want to take up our cross daily to follow him who found the peace that the world cannot give or take away, which it cannot, in fact, understand, yet whose life has become almost automatically the world's standard, at least in thought, for the most high. Naturally in some instances the rejection of the full claim of right religion to the effect that the most high is also fully the most real comes from sincere intellectual difficulties. It may also come from a heart breaking with sympathy but without ultimate faith and hope.

[3] I Corinthians 2:14-15.

Yet, in the main, it is true that the rejection of religion because of the evil in the world comes far more from those who stand apart from full surrender of their lives than from those who have owned outright the Cross as the center of their life and thinking. The most high judges our desire for perfect pleasure and demands that we find truth on a higher level where suffering is not inconsistent with the experience of the best that this life has to offer. When this best is also our highest standard of truth, God's Agape fellowship, the problem of evil has shifted perspective radically from that of the natural man whose one demand of life is that there be no suffering, that all be pleasure, or else God must be limited.

Suffering as a means is not only not inconsistent with God's Agape; it is almost presupposed by it, theoretically; and, existentially, we start at the Cross, with self-giving love, with voluntary, vicarious suffering, as the best means to effect the highest end. Yet how often and how superficially the hedonistic premise is assumed as a standard that voids the claims of right religious reason. Evil must be defined and dealt with throughout from our highest perspective of truth. We must accordingly first reject outright the hedonistic premise as a major premise and we must thereafter avoid mixing our perspectives. The only legitimate partial power of hedonism is the right to affirm that suffering must be completely excluded as an end. Suffering must not be purposeless.

In the third place, personal experience, the personal-spiritual level, is enriched by selection and variety. This is an important point inasmuch as some feel that the very nature of finite experience precludes a full solution of the problem of evil. Whitehead, for instance, claims that the problem of evil is inherently insoluble because experience means selection and selection means exclusion, that is, the elimination or the rejection of some good. All experience is, anyway, he points out, the destruction of the integral unity of past selections for the sake of a new selection. Repetition or confirmation in feeling is even that, he says, part of another experience in which the previous meaning as such, as the occasion of absolute self-enjoyment, has already been destroyed. We not only "murder to dissect," making public knowledge in any fullness impossible, but we also murder to live. We have to keep killing the past. We must destroy even ourselves to keep alive. The verdure of the present is ever nourished on the corpses of our own pasts.

The objective evil in the universe, Whitehead claims, is due to the nature of the process itself. Every infinitude requires a finitude of realization in which certain elements are necessarily destroyed. Novelty of experience which is necessary to its continued richness, its progressive achievement, involves the destruction of what is, and that destruction is that far tragedy, and that far evil. The perpetual perishing of the world is an inevitable evil accompanying process. The greatest evil is, of course, subjective, where there is destruction of the highest form of beauty achieved, the missing of the greatest possibilities open to the individual or to society.

Objective evil, nevertheless, is important. Whitehead himself sums up this objective nature of evil under three principles: "1. that all actualization is finite; 2. that finitude involves the exclusion of alternate possibility; 3. that mental functioning introduces into realization subjective forms conformal to relevant alternatives excluded from the completeness of physical realization."[4] Novelty means exclusion; exclusion means destruction; destruction is evil. All life involves passage, and this passage is by its very nature destructive. Even in eternity there cannot, therefore, be life without evil. God is continually creating, being an eternal principle of concretion. All concretion involves finitude and finitude is inevitably evil.

This objection must be faced head on. Whitehead's idea of destruction as the inevitable concomitant of novelty seems mostly mathematical in nature, and therefore not applicable to the fullness of experience. It is an illicit transfer of the problems of one

[4] *Adventures of Ideas*, p. 233.

perspective to those of another. That is why the solution, in fact, can be had only on the personal-spiritual plane. In experience the good does not require either its total or its invariable exemplification. The exclusion involved in contrast is the foundation even of aesthetics. Whitehead himself stresses this. Massiveness wearies; and monotony reduces the grade of experience. The change from one contrast to another enhances the pleasure of the total experience. It is in the composition and in the exemplification of contrasts, not in the fact of mere exclusiveness or lack of universality, that evil is produced. Evil is a false composition of experience. If that evil is eliminated, novelty does not mean loss; but selectivity, on the very contrary, means heightened pleasure, deepened sensitivity, enriched experience. It is, therefore, not necessary to appeal for a solution to God's complete nature, which can synthesize our fragmentary and broken experiences. Forms, though small, can be perfect. The Greeks, in fact, called the formless, the unlimited, the imperfect. Perfection in the personal realm may be relative. A small glass may be full even though small. A snowflake does not have to be a snow-capped mountain, filling all, to be perfect. It can be perfect as a snowflake.

Perfection is too often confused with mere size or with mere inclusiveness. Even in mechanics there can be the change of form, as from the circle to the spiral, as A. E. Taylor points out in his commentary on Plato's "Timaeus," without destruction of the beauty of the form. Energy can change from pattern to pattern, as in growth, without there being any loss because the pattern is changed. And if loss is defined arithmetically, and it need not be, must not be in this instance, this loss does not necessarily involve evil in experience.

Within a fellowship of infinite participants, or at least of an uncountable number from our standpoint, there can be indefinite novelty without loss. Those who think eternity must be either varied because of loss or else without novelty have hardly waked up to live. Consider even the case of a farm. It used to be thought necessary for a piece of land to lie fallow for one out of seven years in order to recuperate and to bear better crops. With the modern knowledge of the variation of crops, however, the fields bear abundantly without either fallow periods or loss of fertility. The variation is enough to relieve the monotony and to supply the needed nitrogen. Novelty depends upon *good variation*, not upon *evil loss*.

We must be clear on this point. We must not fall prey to illegitimate analogies. We must not mix our perspectives. The new does not have to mean loss to experience. Even God creates to make things new. He likes the new. "Behold, I make all things new."[5] That is what, in our history, He is ever about. Nor does mere increase satisfy Him or us. Creativity means change, rearrangement, variety, novelty. The housewife's instinct to rearrange the furniture has something divine, as well as something demonic (restlessness), in it! It is not evil that we cannot now at this moment have every kind of experience. Even God does not have that. That is a mathematical abstraction straight from the mathematical blackboard. It is not evil that we shall never become the one and only God with all the experience that He can have. There is no evil *per se* in finitude. Goodness is according to nature; it is according to measure. Existentially speaking we may blame more on our finitude than we should. Or is it perhaps a lack of humility, a false deification of ourselves in desire, that makes us call our finitude evil? Is there a subtle pride in assuming for ourselves in desire all the experience there is, perhaps an over-seriousness in us which makes us take up, at least in thought, not only our own cross but God's?

No, goodness is according to size and specific individuation. It is not evil that one pickerel is not all the pickerel there are, possessing the possibility of all their combined experiences. "If all the axes were one axe," is a pleasant children's ditty, but not a theological condition. It is not evil, even, that the flounder is not a pickerel. Let him wonder about it, as the old Swedish proverb has it, but let

[5] Revelation 21:5.

him wonder as a flounder. That I have to leave my wife and children this morning to labor in my study is not by itself evil. The picture of a bee on a flower forever sucking honey may please some. Yet it seems more satisfactory to the bee, probably, also to fly in the air, to crawl on the flower, to swarm with the hive.

By going away and coming back, with hard work and thought in between, we enrich and deepen our common life. Always to hang around for the sake of direct fellowship appeals only to those who lack life. Those who have it have zest for change, for creative variety of experience, for a widening and deepening of fellowship. Jesus' prediction that there will be no marriage in heaven must mean not a lessening of intensive fellowship, but an extending of it. God wants more than worship from us—direct experience. He also wants work—indirect experience. Finitude for the finite is by itself no evil. The only question is if by a fuller and better relation to the infinite that finitude can become completely satisfactory. That is a matter of personal experience. Our best moments here, the pinnacles of our joy, thunder the affirmative answer. Even ordinary life at its very best is extremely pleasant. Life can be good beyond description at every level of experience. Yet the intensity and the rapture of the mystic moment when God speaks to our soul is beyond compare. And here we have only the slightest foretaste. Who can say if heaven is the extension and development of our very best on earth, *beyond compare*, that it must be evil because we are not ever infinite?

We shall only mention, in the fourth place, that on the personal-spiritual level there can be no monotony. That has been somewhat brought out incidentally in our last point as we discussed the meaning of selection and exclusion in experience. In heaven, moreover, wherever God's will is perfectly done, there can be no monotony precisely because experience by being selective and exclusive is also creatively enriched and pleasantly varied. We need not resort to any device like a perfect memory to lay the spectre of endless monotony. Why is it, though, that this horrible dread of an endless monotony is widely shared? At least we meet many who say that they dread it. Is this a way to soothe one's aching for immortality when the mind of the natural man finds it hopeless? Is this a case of "sour grapes"? Or is it another way to evade God's call? Is it a way to avoid His demand that we put on immortality in thought and conduct now? Why do some have to insist that unless there is evil to combat in eternity it must be monotonous? Is not our positive experience of God and His fellowship real enough to settle that question immediately? Is it raised by those who dread the reality of perfection judging their lives and therefore cannot endure even to think it or to admit its possibility, even in heaven?

The full life in God's fellowship is characterized by both freedom and creative zest. It is the overflowing joys we share, to use a faltering example, as heedless of time or task we walk with our son or daughter in the brightness of a spring morning. It is like the delight, though incomparably better, of course, of young lovers who linger at the telephone though there is no news to tell. Spiritual communion is inexhaustible. The college sophomore may feel that he has exhausted the personalities of his professors. The professors usually know that they have not even begun to understand the sophomore.

The media of the Christian fellowship are the endless resources of the eternal God. The richer life becomes, the deeper and more satisfying the fellowship. Von Hügel and A. E. Taylor like to think of love as perfect in heaven while there is an internal growth in the knowledge of God which keeps on forever. Increase in knowledge thus relieves the monotony and provides an adequate principle of novelty. This may all be so, but surely it is not needed to keep heaven interesting. As an argument against monotony, at least, this is an unnecessary compromise with the objection. The experience of the infinite fellowship is never boredom; weariness is of the flesh. The vision of God can be meaningless and monotonous only to those who have had no time-transcending experience of it.

In questions like these it is hard, in fact, for an existential thinker to be sufficiently patient with the speculative philosopher. He finds it really difficult to understand why abstract ideas of perfection without relevance to normal experience are even brought into the discussion. Yet he must examine them patiently to see if there is any reason in what we know why evil can never be solved. The solution of moral evil *existentially* means, however, Can I be saved? Will those dear to me be saved? If all that lives is dear to me, or if I understand that justice or the fullest redemptive activity is not done unless all are saved, the question becomes, Will all be saved? Or the question can be put this way: Unless God is of such a nature as to save all, will He save me? Unless evil is totally overcome will I ever overcome it? The more shallow the person, of course, the more shallow is his existential question. The deeper and more universal the person, the deeper and more universal are also his existential concerns. Yet if all can ever be made as deeply and as creatively happy as they can be, far even beyond what we can here want or think, it seems quibbling to talk about evil as the perpetual frustration of experience because selection means loss and lack of loss means monotony.

Give us our deepest and most beautiful satisfaction creatively and zestfully varied, challenge it with ever more abundant life, and extend it to all life that ever lived, and then talk about the perpetual tragedy of time's perpetually perishing! Talk it is. No more. To the zestful life, change and creative variety mean life and life more abundantly. It means increase in satisfaction. It means indescribable enjoyment. Those who have known it on a high level, even for a moment, know that all life seems concentrated in it. One moment of religious peace, of positive, rich peace, with God at the center, is such that words actually do fail us. Those who have known it can say with Paul: "I am filled with comfort; I overflow with joy in all our affliction."[6] Before the reality of such a positive peace speculative questions become trivial.

[6] II Corinthians 7:4.

CHAPTER V

Evil and Freedom

In the fifth place, on the personal level, with Christ as the content of the kind of perfect life that we have actually seen, freedom takes on fuller and deeper meaning. We have been given freedom in order to become real persons, sons, not automata. God shares with us His own nature. We are made in His very image. In order that our freedom might become real we have been given a will to live which contains a will to independence. In our innermost natures, as given to us in our creation, we have a drive to self set over against a drive toward others. We have been given a will to self-preservation and a will to social life, a will to self-perpetuation and a will to community. God wants us to be free, to be ourselves, to have a certain independence for and by ourselves. He wants us to be individuals, to be different, to be new representations. God is creative. He wants us to share His never ceasing creative fullness. He has made us both free and responsible. He has made us both for ourselves and for Himself. Not that He is selfish, but the good must relate itself inevitably to its Source. Apart from this Source it cannot ever exist. Since all our good comes from Him and since we are on the level of free beings, on the personal-spiritual level, we can only reach and maintain our perfection according to our measure by receiving fully from Him. It is for our best, as well as according to His nature, that to be good we must all share in the Prime Source of the Good.

This is the situation, however, which gives evil its meaning, both on the social and on the natural level. The social divides into two parts: our relation to God and our relation to others. Our freedom is the key to the world's evil.[1] To become really free we must act in rebellion against others; we must act distinctly as separate individuals; we must sometime or other go contrary to their decisions. This may not eventuate in overt action. It may remain a hidden holding-off from others, and an inner judgment of them. Yet unless we exercise our independent judgment, unless we put ourselves in the seat of responsibility; unless we assume the power and the right to decide for ourselves what is right; unless we rebel in this sense against all authority, both individual and collective, we can never become true selves. To eat of the tree of knowledge is necessarily to want to become like God. We must assume God's place; we must be fully free in our decision if we are to become real individuals. Spiritual and ethical autonomy is a necessary stage to true selfhood. Apart from this stage freedom never becomes real, mature, and effective. God wants sons, not automata. God wants free sons who willingly love Him and who serve Him because they have come to themselves. The freedom that God gives us is no farce. It is both real and full.

Yet God also made us for fellowship. The content of our freedom can never satisfy us unless we live in positive, open fellowship with both God and men. Rebellion against God is necessary at some point in our lives if we are to become free sons, glorifying Him out of love and gratitude. The time must come when we choose for ourselves, judging even God. The time must come when the children stop adoring their parents in unquestioning obedience and begin to look them over in the light of their own understanding. They must judge their parents. The wise parents rejoice in this sign of maturity in the children's eyes.

[1] With regard to natural evil we shall see that this is true both in nature's bearing on life and as an evolutionary background of life, through the animal world, fulfilled only on the level of personal-spiritual life.

Thus every man, if he is not to remain an animal, if he is to rise to moral decision, revolts against God, hides from Him, questions Him, perhaps even hates Him. Every man must pick of the forbidden tree and be banished from the garden of innocence. Every man makes fig leaves behind which to hide his nakedness when God walks in the garden. This rebellion underlies sin. Sin is our refusal to want to know God's will, to affirm as right what we know of it, and to act according to it. Sin is both direct and indirect. It is *indirectly* the refusal to treat others and nature as we know God would have us. All we do, in the end, is for or against God.

Directly sin is defiance of God's will for us. Sin is whatever thwarts willingly, with our consent in act or state, God's purpose for Christian fellowship, according to our highest available understanding of it. Evil is *all* that thwarts this purpose in any way whatever. Evil is thus defined in terms of our historic time and of means, not in terms of eternity or of ends. Sin is as direct a rebellion against God's will as a historic creature is capable of. All have to rebel against God, at least in temptation, in order to become free, to become real selves, to become willing sons who know why they have chosen to be adopted into the family of God.

This includes Jesus. God "made him to be sin for us."[2] He himself knew that none was fully and spontaneously good but God. Through crying and tears he had to become delivered from death, and that not only from physical death but from the death of sin which tempted him. Exactly what he went through, whether he actually rebelled sinfully, we do not know. We cannot explain the Bible at this point because we cannot find clear light. He is claimed to have been tempted in all things yet to have been without sin. He also seems to have been conscious that God alone was good. On this point no proof-text will do. No one can now know the consciousness of Jesus. When he cried out that no one could

[2] II Corinthians 5:21.

convict him of any sin he surely was using sin in the sense of the people, that which could be known, a public infraction of the law. This much we feel confident to say, that we know that he knew the power of temptation, the power of a will to self contrary to God's will. The temptations in the wilderness were real. "Not my will, but thy will" was the cry of an agonized experience. Whether or not he ever defied or hid God's full will we cannot know.

It is easy to make Jesus into an unhistorical myth at this point. We do know that he struggled with God, making the content of his freedom real. He became a willing son who must be about his Father's business. We do know that he was tempted in all things even as we are, and that he understands from within our infirmities. He is within our history, not outside it. He is a true and fully actual event that can typify and mediate. Decisively we do know that he so dominantly accepted God's full will for him that his life has become the light of men, both the wisdom and the power of God for our salvation. We must not make Jesus either a predetermined person without freedom to sin or a sinless abstraction of our reverence. He must be our friend, challenger, and comforter, history's freely won, living triumph over sin.

The sooner and more fully the sons can come to know the Father's will and accept it freely for themselves, the better it is. Jesus is our pioneer, the first-born among many brethren. Most men, however, wander far off into strange countries and take a long time to come to themselves. When they do, they return to their Father and home. Some turn off elsewhere on the way; some leave home more than once. The history of man, however, is amazingly the history of his individual and collective fleeing from God. Our earthly history is mostly the stage of our eating of the tree that opens our eyes to good and evil, that makes us crave to decide for ourselves; that fills us with both the fear and the thrill of our attempted self-sufficiency. Yet God has so made us and our history that we must all pass through this stage of attempted self-sufficiency, through self-despair, to God's security and therein to true freedom. We are made for God and cannot ever be free except within His will. That is the decree of His goodness. The Father knows best. The Father wants the best for us and is ready to give it to us when we are ready to receive it understandingly, willingly, trustingly.

Evil is basically due to the necessity of our rebellion, at least in temptation, that we might be free; our estrangement that we might understand; our hate and hiding that we might love. How patient and good God is! For our sake He lets us revolt. Evil is also due to the consequences that must follow our rebellion in order to show us that God's way is best. We are free to differ, free to try our own ways, free to run off into the far country and there to waste our inheritance on our selfish pleasures. But we are not free to escape the hunger and the loneliness and the sense of guilt that follow. We are not free to avoid fear and trouble. We are not free to be satisfied in our chosen situation. We are free to make ourselves good, but we are then not free to feel free from our cosmic responsibility and dread. Evil is the barbs on the fences as we climb away from the good which God in His mercy has prepared for us. What we call evil is thus a good means in God's hand. The farther we go the thicker and the longer the barbs, and there is a point beyond which we cannot go. Yet the barbs at the beginning are never so thick and so sharp as to discourage us from examining for ourselves what seem the pleasant playgrounds beyond God's purpose. Evil is the electric stick that shocks the ant when it wants to go in the direction of its own destruction. Yet these figures fall far short of the wonder whereby God matches evil and freedom in such a way that we can become both intelligently free and gratefully willing to accept His way, which is best for us. Our metaphysical freedom is in order to attain spiritual freedom. Freedom to be real involves evil, at least the evil of temporary estrangement, but such evil is through and through for our own good.[3] Evil is a fact real to us but also good for us, good as a means but not as an end. Evil is evil only as ends become means and means become ends. Evil is real with and for freedom. That it be, as a whole, is good; that it be *no more,* nevertheless, is far better.

Man's need to be himself, to be free, to act autonomously, also makes him put himself at the center with respect to others. God has given us a will to live, a drive to self-preservation, an urge to independence and individuality. This makes us want to be self-sufficient. Yet he has also put us in a world with others who want to be independent, too. Thus with limited knowledge, a knowledge purposely limited according to our right measure, we get ourselves into conflicts. Men want each other; they want to be loved and to be appreciated by one another. Yet they also want to be themselves untrammeled by the choices of others. To get unity in their personal universe they even want to make choices for others.

The stronger of these drives within us is the will to self. As we grow up our natural and easiest course of action is to insist on our own will. Thus when conflicts arise we want our own way. We make others the means to our own satisfaction. We do not enter into their position to judge even fairly from their angle. Often we thoughtlessly live from day to day simply following out in life what we ourselves want. We may even say, "Lord, Lord," and yet not *do* His will, accepting the fellowship status. Others refuse, too, and thus the evils of conflict are on.

We also tend naturally to measure our satisfaction in terms of what others enjoy or have. Thus arise ill wills in that each wants as much as the other and more. At the same time we both love and hate. We trust and are suspicious. We fear and have faith. We have fellowship but cannot let ourselves go. We are made

[3] The full relation between these means and ends will most likely remain beyond historic observation. Otherwise we might suspect that we have made God's ways ours, and have thereby become Ptolemaic in our theology.

that way by God to become truly free as selves within a living fellowship.

One aspect of this conflict is deep fear and a sense of guilt. We want both freedom and security. We want both to be independent and to belong. We have a drive for security and a drive for society. We want to be wholly ourselves, without let or hindrance, self-sufficient, yet also loved and needed. Self-security is our deepest original drive. Yet we can never become self-secure. The most boastful attempt to feel so mocks us. God has given us but a moment of time. All float down the river of life toward death. The waterfalls that shatter every boat are ahead of us all. As a matter of fact the indentations of the falls reach far enough in to make some fall as soon as they begin to live, and many all around us go over the falls from time to time long before our own age. We live in a world constantly threatened with death. We have no final resting place. No plan is definite. Everything is precarious. No hope is sure. Thus a basic insecurity undercuts all finite freedom. We have no control over the end. We know, deep down, that we are in no way self-sufficient. The fear of death is a depth-fact, a subconscious reality, in every life. Fear makes for frenzy. We lose our inner calm. Outwardly we may seem relaxed, but there is a deep, hidden tension. Our overt fears are but the incidental contents of our death-deep anxiety. All depth-thinking is existential thinking over against the fear of death. Let us step accidentally or thoughtlessly into the path of a passing automobile and we feel our hearts beat. Panic is nearer to many than they think. It is a dark background of their life making them feel constantly insecure.

This anxiety is also due to the fear of God. We know that we are cosmically responsible. We may mock it, deny it, try to explain it away. Yet the sense of right hangs over all normal human beings. This is no mere sense of need to adjust to society. Some who are most "adjusted" feel uneasy about God. It is rooted in our existential situation. Freedom involves responsibility. The more freedom we assume the more responsible we become; and if we evade it we are also responsible for that. Thus we know ourselves guilty. We know that we have no right to be at the center. We know that others have as much right as we. We may even know that we are responsible for them, that their misfortune and blood cry to God against us. Thus we are guilty. We sense it in depth-awareness.

Besides, we have a fear of the unknown which is mixed up with our fear both of death and of the God we know. The God with a dark face stands behind the lighted face of Christ. We should like to see the future; we should like to plan with definiteness, under secure conditions. We cannot. We should like to know the ultimate in all its being, meaning, and possible acting; then we should know to what extent we can and cannot do certain things. We cannot thus know God except as fully adopted sons. Thus we are anxious. Anxiety becomes clothed with concrete fears. Fears keep reminding us of our constant insecurity.

This insecurity colors the use of our freedom. We try to grasp things, to gather possessions, to have steady income in order to feel independent. Greed is linked up with our basic anxiety, with our attempt to feel secure, with our attempt, however false, at self-security. The trait may become partly autonomous, of course, an end for its own sake beyond our awareness of insecurity. We feel no more secure basically. We know that. Yet things enhance our prestige among others. Pride is self-bloating aimed at self-security. We become proud of what we have. We become lovers of pleasures, of the things we can enjoy. Pleasures can slake, we hope, for the time being our thirst for secure satisfaction.

We are then perhaps also proud over being able to afford them. We compare ourselves with others, again, to feel ourselves socially secure. Possessions seem to help. Position seems to help. Thinking as others do seems to help. Thus we conform to social standards. We commit the sin of conventionality. Or else we want to impress others with our difference, with our individuality. That may make us seem secure, as though we knew what it is all about. We cannot make up our minds. We want both to be the same as others and yet also to be different. We want them to like us, and yet we want to be ourselves, often aggressively, which makes them dislike us, feel fearful, feel insecure.

We want to "show off" to impress them even while we are half-conscious that they will dislike us. Or we want to adjust completely, keeping our ideas and achievements to ourselves, and we thereupon despise ourselves for forfeiting our freedom, our independence. In that way, too, we feel frustrated and futile. In all this, moreover, we feel a sense of guilt, a fear of God for the way we live with others. We feel insecure.

In our own insecurity we may even take pleasure in the insecurity of others. Somehow that may make us, or seems to make us, feel relatively secure. If we ourselves are insecure we tend to dislike especially people who are sure of themselves. This is particularly true if the sureness is defensive. The dogmatic kind of sureness is often the mind which fear has closed. We may dislike the person also who has found security beyond himself. He may seem either a hypocrite or naïve. At the same time in one corner of our lives we may treasure the man of faith. We may cling to him in order to feel the warmth of his security. The world follows those who are authentically secure. If they cannot be found, the world may make a golden calf of the partial security of any man who is lost in a cause that is big enough to offer something to live for, to give a sense of security or worth to life. Yet even while we thus admire the man of faith, one side of us may still want to hurt others. We may feel alternately genuine warmth toward someone and then dislike welling up in us simply because we are still insecure. Security is never collective. It is never vicarious, except in appearance or suggestion. Here each one must be an individual. In this sense the individual of Kierkegaard's existential moment is the religious man.

The fearful are naturally the most aggressive. They are also the most proud. Pride is a front, an attempt to feel superior in security. Watch the youth that swaggers! Pride is fooling oneself with the inner feeling of strength and merit, by throwing out one's chest and throwing back one's head to make others shrink, or at least to keep them from hurting us, from sensing our weakness. Pride acts differently from the normal straightening out of our bodies. Pride is self-conscious. Pride is tense, brittle. Pride is fear's fortification from within, but it is false front, leaving us vulnerable to the weakest enemy—a slur, a sneer, even a false report.

Or we may become falsely humble. True humility has the dignity of perfect security beyond our own worth and strength. Perfect humility is the experience of complete dependence and complete security in God. The humility of fear is irrational cringing. It is akin to superstition. It is fear of the fall which cometh after pride. Fear underlies the false pacifism which shudders sentimentally at the constructive use of force. Fear's pacifism does away with an angry and punishing God. Fear's pacifism is the hiding from the real world by means of an imagined one. True pacifism is the strength of a peace not our own.

True pacifism is the allaying of fears, not by word, but by an inner security which has overcome suffering and death. Strange are the ways of men. Strangely mixed are our feelings. Who can understand even himself? Yet freedom we want, and fellowship, and both need a common ground, security and direction in the eternal and the absolute, in the Christian God who overcomes evil, openly triumphing over it.

Fear of death, of the unknown, of the God we know, of others, seizes us at the very depths of our beings, and we suppress it. We are busy. We try to do good. We wonder and worry whether we really do good. We worry, deep down, whether God is pleased with us, whether we can get by with what we are doing. Our freedom is thus filled and colored with fear. God wants us both to be free and to have fellowship with him and with our fellow men.

Nothing less will overcome evil. Yet the process of producing this fellowship is long and hard. It is costly. It is full of evil. It is no artificial fiat. It is the struggle at the depths of our being for inwardness and sociality, for individuality and godliness. Only by the understanding of the nature, the seriousness, and the glory of our freedom as we emerge, painfully and joyfully both, through struggle to see and to do God's will, can we ever explain the nature of freedom.

Freedom is for positive content. It is goodness which leads us to repentance. Goodness uses severity. Severity is necessary to make us think, to make us rethink our lives. Hunger will stop the prodigal's career. Yet unless in reality the good were more satisfactory than evil, unless we could come to ourselves, our truer selves, unless our eyes could be opened to make us see that we have been blind, there would be no real freedom. God would then be forcing us. That is why no illustration about the barbed wire or about an ant and a stick will fully do.

We must rise to the personal-spiritual level. Only the thoughtful understanding that God's way is best for us and that His goodness is our deepest satisfaction can make us willingly accept it. God's peace is not the absence of pain, not the final surrender to His will because of the terrors that evil will bring. It is the willing, understanding acceptance by free sons of the Father's will as best for them and for all, which only the judgment of it by the children independently can effect.

CHAPTER VI

Evil and Sin

Before we leave this social side of evil in relation both to God and to others we must ask two questions: (1) Are we not making light of sin? (2) Does our explanation not mean that God planned and is responsible for our sin?

As to the first question, if taking sin seriously enough means blind fear of God, terror of His judgment, cringing before His punishment, the horror of primitive taboo before His uncanny holiness; if sin is absolute in the sense that even to try to think about right and wrong from God's perspective is to blaspheme in the sense that the very attempt to understand the Father's will is itself a making light of it; if sin is the failure of the finite being to fulfill an infinite responsibility of which by nature he is qualitatively incapable—if such interpretations of sin are rightly serious, then indeed we do take it lightly. We believe that the father who demands blind obedience from his children, who makes them the slaves of his rage if they fail to obey his will, instantly and unquestioningly, is not fit to be our symbol for God.

We believe, rather, that the best that we know, the most high, is the most real. The Father of the Prodigal Son is for us a far better example. The wise and patient parent who loves his children enough to let them have freedom to question both his motives and his actions, who lets them ask and find out the why of the father's discipline, who has them grow up loving, willing, under-

43

standing, and anxious out of a free, responsible concern to obey the rules for the family because they know that they are the best rules for the family fellowship as a whole including the last and least member of it—that parent is a better index of what God is than he who demands an unquestioning obedience and is insulted even if his motives and actions are questioned. In the light of the relation to the better parent, sin takes on a deeper hue. It is not now terrible because of some mysterious decree that cannot be broken without unspeakable retribution; sin is not now awful because we are inescapably caught in it and cannot escape the guilt for it except by some irrational self-humiliation and arbitrary, paradoxical forgiveness. Sin is now, rather, the wounding of our deepest self in our deepest affections and desires.

Sin is the perverted thwarting of our most basic needs and of our most serious longings. Sin is the letting ourselves be pulled down by the weight of our desire, a weight given to us by God, an adversary, the Devil, the *id* against the *ego*, with the intent to be free for ourselves in order to be ourselves, when something else within and without tells us more basically that we cannot be free as ourselves until we let ourselves by the power of God be freed within God's fellowship. Sin becomes our worst enemy because God is our best friend. Sin is the perversion of our essential selves. Sin is the thwarting, the arresting, of the development of the self as a free son, by the starving of the self away from the happy home that awaits us, and away from the Father who runs to meet us whenever we are ready to go home. Sin is our finding, and letting ourselves be dominated by—indeed, our helping to make—a society that does not satisfy. Sin is our wronging God by refusing His fellowship, which alone can fully satisfy us. It is simply wrong, it is, indeed, to wrong God, to think that He holds the finite creature responsible for the infinite law, that he attributes infinite guilt for finite infraction, that the relative can sin absolutely, even though of relative capacity in wisdom and will, simply because the sin is against the absolute. Finite transgression merits a finite guilt; finite capacity involves finite responsibility; finite wrong deserves finite retribution—on the level of justice. And God must at least be just. We must, then, on this level, treat the relative as relative, and not make it absolute in order by specious reasoning to impress on ourselves the seriousness of sin.

Christian faith, however, is not on the level of God's justice. If God makes us responsible for the keeping of the whole law beyond our sufficiency to do so, it is only because He wants us to be delivered from our false attempt at self-sufficiency; He wants to take us out of our circle of self, out of our slavery to self, into the glorious liberty of the sons of God, where we live by a faith and a power not our own for the sake of a common Father and a common fellowship. God makes the law impossible in order that being convicted by it we may find no way to live by it.

God does not primarily want servants of the law, but free sons, eager for right relations. The law in this respect is only a tutor unto Christ. Only by our getting beyond the whole perspective of the law, clean and clear away from this juridical point of view or attitude, into the understanding and acceptance of the divine Agape where there is no question of law or of trespasses, but of love and of joy, of peace and of creative personal relations through the power of God, can we ever be set fully free.

This question is, indeed, crucial. Those who reject God's fellowship on the basis of His own Agape must not be comforted by His love. For them there is no escape so long as they neglect "so great a salvation." They must see and dread the law as a tyrannical enemy over against them. The Gospel is for the penitent only. There is no Gospel for those who wilfully persist in sin. The goodness of God (in the form of severity) must lead them to the repentance of sin and of dead works. To them God is not the One who forgives but the One who never forgives until the last farthing has been paid; and for them that is *never* so long as they persist in living under the law. Over them, as such, abides forever the wrath of God. Existentially this is true.

Luther, in this perspective, is indeed right:

> But it is a Thing very strange and unknown to the World, to teach Christians to learn to be ignorant of the Law, and so to live before God, as if there were no Law: notwithstanding, except thou be ignorant of the Law, and be assuredly persuaded in thine Heart that there is now no Law nor Wrath of God, but altogether Grace and Mercy for Christ's sake, thou canst not be saved: for by the Law cometh the Knowledge of Sin. Contrariwise, Works and the keeping of the Law must be so straitly required in the World, as if there were no Promise of Grace: and that because of the stubborn, proud, and hard-hearted, before Whose Eyes nothing must be set but the Law, that they may be terrified and humbled. For the Law is given to terrify and kill such, and to exercise the Old Man: and both the Word of Grace and of Wrath, must be rightly divided according to the Apostle, 2 Tim. ii.[1]

Yet though the natural man receiveth not and cannot know these things because they are spiritually judged, in the light of the Gospel, we can "play the cunning Logician, and make the right Division."[2] In that light we can see the function of the law beyond our ability to keep it. This function is pedagogical rather than punitive. We are not under an impossible demand for the sake of obtaining an arbitrary grace. No flesh may glory before God, not because God is jealous of His own glory after the manner of evil men, or in the manner fearful men attribute such motives to those who have power over them, but because God's glory unites all men in the fellowship which is beyond individual glory and glorying. Grace is not a primary word eternally, only existentially. God's love goes before and behind our background of sin. Redemption is not a primary word eternally, only existentially. Fellowship is the eternal word, the fellowship of God. Not the

[1] *A Commentary on St. Paul's Epistle to the Galatians*, (London, 1760). pp. 18-19.
[2] *Ibid.*, p. 22.

juridical but the family perspective is central to Christian faith.

The personal-spiritual perspective of God's love is the inner-most sanctuary of interpretation. Hence Berdyaev is right in placing the ethics of creativeness after redemption. Redemption is a stage, a means, a pointing to something beyond itself. Reconciliation is for the sake of the restored fellowship. Sin is thus not an eternal category demanding that it be beyond interpretation. The goodness of God is incommensurate with man's sin and the power of His love incommensurate with the power of sin. "The long-suffering of our Lord is salvation";[3] His patience is His faithfulness to our freedom; His slowness is His humility and the sign of His strength. Sin is taken most seriously, as far as explanation goes, not when we limit the explanation to our existential urgency, but when we see all things in the light of God's highest revelation to us.

We are in an impossible situation under the law because we ourselves have chosen to be there, and God will not let us stay in that situation. We have chosen to live under the law in our own strength for the sake of a false self-security, an illusory self-sufficiency, a deceiving autonomy. We have done this only after we have found out, in understanding and experience, that to live at the expense of others, to be our own law, is impossible, after we have discovered that other people similarly wanted to live at our expense, be their own law, too. We have therefore chosen the law as a neutral arbiter among us all. By means of the law of universally right relations we thought that we could all be autonomous, none having by means of it to surrender his individual independence.

But God never gave us the strength to be free for ourselves even within the law. He made us for fellowship on the basis of creative love and co-operation. He made us so as to need others and above all so as to need Him. The law therefore convicted us of our weakness, and sin slew our self-sufficiency. Its guilt

[3] II Peter 3:15.

robbed us of our wanted freedom, imprisoning us beyond our power ever to escape by our own wisdom and goodness. Sin is thus our master; we are its slaves; until God sets us free through faith in His own self and fellowship. Sin is therefore as serious existentially as our basic life-situation, but it is the result of a false situation which we have ourselves chosen.

Yet this situation in the light of God's full purpose is not qualitatively different from evil in general. All evil is somehow summed up in sin and can be explained at last in terms of man's sin, in relation to it either directly or indirectly, either as a chronological foreground or as an existential background. On the other hand all sin can be classed basically under the heading and function of evil. Sin is no more an unchangeable fact than is any other evil. As a matter of fact the change is usually, or at least often, more sudden. The fact of sin may make grace the more richly and quickly to abound. Sin is not a permanent situation in the nature of things. Sin is man's direct denial, as direct as is possible to a creature, of God's fellowship for him.

Yet such a denial deepens his individuality and enriches his freedom. Existentially it is wrong that we allow sin to reign the least bit in our lives. From the point of view of the fuller explanation of God's purpose to create fellowship we can see and own its function. Sin now is a blend of self-will and weakness, ignorance, and external temptation. Sin is not apart from evil in general. Sin is the yielding to the evil which besets us. Yet it need neither "reign" nor "remain."[4] Though it remain after it has stopped reigning, God can and does in His time as we yield ourselves fully also take away the root of it in us, as well as give us at last a new heaven and a new earth. We do take sin seriously. How can we help it and care? Yet what is most important is that we take God most seriously, that He be all in all, that our highest perspective of truth be allowed to shine everywhere without restriction or taboo.

[4] Cf. Wesley, *Works,* Vol. I, Ser. XIII, p. 113.

Does this view not mean that God is responsible for our sin?
Yes, and no. God cannot sin by nature. He does not want to revolt against His own perfect self. He wants, rather, to share His
own Agape. He wants only the best for all. Yet He did create this
kind of world and He knew what He was doing. This is the kind
of world to effect Christian fellowship. He not only allowed us
a neutral freedom, but gave us purposefully a freedom weighted
toward the self, toward estrangement, toward maturing self-judg-
ment, toward an independence that would make our freedom
authentic. Besides, He put us in a precarious environment. Even
the Garden of Eden story represents man's fall as due to three
conditions not of man's own choosing: a forbidden tree, a desire
for the fruit, and an external tempter to seduce man. The Garden
of Man never was, and never is, a neutral freedom. There is a
heavy weight of evil on history, a drag of evil on human life. It
is not just as easy naturally to be God-centered as self-centered,
and that is the way all men *must* begin. This, too, is God's planned
way of salvation.

Unless God purposed this kind of world, including man's rebellion, the Cross of Christ becomes accidental as a full principle
of explanation, devotion, purpose, and power. The story of Jesus
is then, indeed, pushed to the edge of interpretation. The Bible
speaks of an eternal purpose which God purposed in Christ Jesus.
This means that He foresaw and intended this kind of world as
the perfect means for the perfect end of the Agape fellowship.
The world as a total condition, in its general nature, is not perfect
as an end, but as a means. This is the right kind of world to grow
the Christian fellowship.

The Cross of Christ is the most inclusive and conclusive symbol
and actualization of God's self-giving love where man's rebellion
is canceled as men come to understand why they are born and to
be constrained by the love which sets them gloriously free for fellowship. The Cross, the self-giving of the best because the best is
by nature self-giving, summarizes the story of God's way to effect

the Christian community. Unless there is sin, grace has no meaning. Unless there is sin, love is never seen in its fullest depth. If we start with the highest selective actual, God's love in Jesus Christ, as the truth which most fully satisfies our theoretical and practical problems, individually and socially, we start also insolubly with the background of man's sin. High Calvinism does not hesitate to make the sovereignty of God effect this kind of world. If only its ending were different. Great mystics like Meister Eckhardt[5] have not hesitated to see God's work everywhere, even in connection with sin.

Luther, too, had visions of the full working of God, using even sin and the Devil:

> This I maintain and insist, that God, when he works without the spirit's grace, works everything in everyone, even in the ungodly, in that he alone with his omnipotent moving power sets in motion, drives, and carries with him all that he alone has created, this power, which the created one cannot escape or change, but must necessarily follow and obey, each according to the measure, given of God. Thus even all the ungodly cooperate with him.[6]
>
> Since therefore God drives and works everything in everyone, he also drives and works necessarily even in Satan and the ungodly.[7]

This naturally goes beyond our point of view, not leaving enough recognition to man's freedom, at least in emphasis, and yet even man's power to sin is given him constantly by God. We know no self-existent human being. We know nothing of men not dependent from moment to moment on God's sustaining activity. In this sense then God participates in our sin, lets us revolt

---

[5] "The Book of Divine Comfort," p. 50, in Blakney's *Meister Eckhart.*

[6] W. A. XVIII, 753, 11, 28 ff., cited by Bring, *Dualism hos Luther,* p. 265, used by Edgar M. Carlson, in "The Theology of Luther according to Swedish Research," *Journal of Religion,* Oct., 1945, p. 247.

[7] W. A. XVIII, 711, 4 ff. in Bring, *Ibid.,* translation mine.

against Him that we might come to understand and love Him the
better and accept His purpose for us.

God Himself does not sin; He cannot do so by nature. Yet He
made a world where men revolt against Him out of a most mixed
situation of weakness, ignorance, the pull of external evil, fear,
self-will, and an acquired evil will, a trait grown partly autonomous, in order that He might make us free, truly free, to be ourselves at length within His goodness, understandingly, gratefully,
creatively. The Cross stands for the depth of God's love and the
height of His wisdom and power. This means of redemption is
no accident. It is central in God's plan. The Cross presupposes the
presence of sin in the world. Schleiermacher had here a pregnant
insight:

> As in our self-consciousness sin and grace are opposed to each
> other, God cannot be thought of as the Author of sin in the same
> sense as that in which He is the Author of redemption. But as
> we never have a consciousness of grace without a consciousness
> of sin, we must also assert that the existence of sin alongside of
> grace is ordained for us by God.[8]

The effecting of the Christian fellowship is the meaning of
process, the highest truth that we know. We need to know that
this is grown in real experience, not manufactured, or bid into
being. We need, therefore, in Christian theology the sense of what
the Mutazilites called "necessary grace" and "the relatively necessary."[9] The effecting of God's goodness in history is due to
the necessary grace of His nature which includes the relative
necessity of man's estrangement and reconciliation.

Grace is at the heart of God. A love without a burden and a
burden without suffering would mean no deep love. The sharing of
the burden and sorrow must at least be a stage in the effecting of
the fellowship that goes deep. To be free man must rebel. The

---

[8] *The Christian Faith*, p. 326.
[9] Moore, *The History of Religions*, Vol. 2, p. 418.

Cross is the necessary grace of God. God must suffer for the ungodly with the godly wherever there is a history of mixed failures, sin and victories. God cannot deny Himself. Even though we are faithless He remains faithful. The faithlessness of some or of all cannot make of no effect the faithfulness of God. "God hath shut up all unto disobedience, that he might have mercy upon all."[10] God foresaw and accepted as a good means human rebellion, and He endures it for our sake and for the joy set before Him. What humility and patience in God to let us share His final joy by letting us rebel against Him and still helping us all the way until we understand and accept His fellowship! He lets us sin one against the other and against Himself and takes up our Cross to show us the end of our suffering. That there be such a world where freedom becomes real, not theoretical, is "relatively necessary." For this end this means is necessary.

Here we have to play "the cunning Logician." Those under the power of sin must fear it, fear God. For them there can be no adequate perspective except the one of the law and of guilt. Yet from the perspective of salvation the spiritual man sees the whole process in a new light. Perhaps we had better not say even from the perspective of salvation because we have left behind the juridical perspective. The idea of salvation is still basically in the juridical perspective. From the perspective of the family fellowship of God we see what a plan and goal our process has for us. We see sin and its needful punishment as a stage toward the fellowship of Agape. We see also beyond this stage how we become filled with gratitude and joy, how the acceptance of God's free, overflowing love makes sin appear as the foolish rebellion of little children against their own father's rules for their own good.

Existentially we must either fear the consequences of sin, its wages, its law, which is death, or we must repudiate its power in overflowing gratitude by means of God's great love which worketh in us mightily. The explanation for its presence in history is,

[10] Romans 11:32.

however, the need for a real rather than a theoretical freedom, that we might become real individuals, free, understanding, willing sons of our Father. God does not cause sin but He made it possible and foresaw it. Sin is of the creature. Perhaps we should get rid of the taboo flavor which is associated with the word and think rather in family terms, in terms of the children's growth and self-development and the periods and attitudes of rebellion or at least candid examination of the patterns which must accompany the reaching of adulthood, the maturation process. The high Christian perspective should share the Father's point of view. Then we are delivered from the false self-seriousness which accompanies existential thinking rooted in actuality or in lesser gods. From this higher perspective we can exclaim with Augustine: "God, through whom the universe, even taken in its sinister side, is perfect. God, from whom things most widely at variance with Thee effect no dissonance, since worser things are included in one plan with better."[11]

"It is the ability of the revelation to save all the past from senselessness that is one of the marks of its revelatory character."[12] Unless we can understand the relatively necessary function of sin in the perfecting of process and explain it through and through in the light of the full purpose of God, we still must fall short of the complete identification of the most high with the most real. The presence of sin is explained by our freedom when we start with the perspective of the Cross, or grace accomplishing its perfect work, even our freedom under God within the Christian fellowship.

[11] Augustine, "Soliloquies," in *The Nicene and Post-Nicene Fathers*, Vol. VII, p. 537.
[12] Richard Niebuhr, *The Meaning of Revelation*, p. 113.

CHAPTER VII

Evil and Nature

Yet even though sin against God, as well as personal and social evil, can be explained in connection with God's purpose to create a free fellowship after His own nature, what of natural evil? What of seemingly senseless destruction in nature apart from the works of men? What of animal pain? To tell the truth, this has long been the writer's most pressing problem, at least intellectually, in connection with the full identification of the most good with the most real. It has, in fact, perplexed us for many long years. History, too, is full of interest in this question of natural evil. Hume, for instance, made it very pointed.[1] Other religions like Hinduism have had a fuller recognition of it than Christian theology, and both in theory, *karma* (the rebirth of all life) and in practice, *ahimsa* (non-injury to any life) have probed and dealt with the problem. Daniel Evans, the writer's learned and thoughtful predecessor, kindly warned us not to deal with it publicly, though he felt that the problem could not be put off in the West for very long. He surely was right that its immediate and direct effect, at least, is not to strengthen faith. Bavinck points out that

> Darwin was led to his agnostic naturalism as much by the misery which he observed in the world as by the facts which scientific investigation brought under his notice. There was too much strife and injustice in the world for him to believe in

[1] Cf. *Dialogues Concerning Natural Religion*, part x.

54

providence and a predetermined goal. A world so full of cruelty and pain he could not reconcile with the omniscience, the omnipotence, the goodness of God.[2]

For a naturalist, too, that cruelty and pain was everywhere observable in nature as well as in history.

Brightman is impressed by the evidence of "surd evils" which have no relation, seemingly, to moral and spiritual maturing. Berdyaev calls the "problem of theodicy" the most tormenting problem of the human consciousness and conscience."[3] Because of the presence of all the suffering there is he believes that "God is certainly not the constructor of the world order, or an administrator of the world whole."[4] He points out that

> Accident plays an immense part in world life and it does not simply indicate lack of knowledge. If a collision takes place between two planets and as a result there is cosmic destruction, that is to say a breach of cosmic harmony, that is something entirely unteleological, and even not necessary, in the sense that there exists no law under which that clash takes place.[5]

Whitehead affirmed in a personal conversation that his weightiest reason for rejecting all full solutions of the problem of evil was not "man's inhumanity to man" but the ruthless character of nature where life devours life without hesitation, stint, or mercy. Joad points to evil in nature, particularly to animal pain, as one strong reason for refusing to accept the full Christian message. C. S. Lewis, after doing his utmost to explain *The Problem of Pain* in the animal world, is still considerably baffled by it. L. J. Henderson writes that "dysteleology is hardly less obvious in nature than teleology, and the search for a final cause of everything is a hopeless task."[6] Schweitzer as a young boy became

[2] Bavinck, *The Philosophy of Revelation*, p. 11.
[3] *Slavery and Freedom*, p. 86.
[4] *Ibid.*, p. 87.
[5] *Ibid.*, p. 99.
[6] *The Order of Nature*, p. 18.

deeply aware of animal pain, in the hunting of birds, and developed his strong doctrine of reverence for life to a large extent out of this awareness. Harnack puts the problem bluntly and negatively: *"It is impossible to give a rational account of nature and history from the standpoint of the grace of experience. For it is absolutely impossible to develop as a rational doctrine the conviction of the transforming grace of God who is also the creator."*[7]

For us to skip lightly over this sixth area would be to be dishonest and to forfeit our rational right to identify as fully as can be the most high and the most real. No full solution may be ours. If so, we must simply and humbly say that at this point whole-response in faith, to the full identification of the most high and the most real, and whole-reason cannot, in this area, go together. Such an admission, if necessary, may be good for both faith and reason. Our faith must live in the power of God and surely that must in the end go far beyond our seeing. Our reason, too, tends to become a substitute for faith, complacent within ourselves, except as we see beyond our fullest horizons the ever rising hills of intellectual difficulty.

Certain things, however, we can say. We can say, for instance, that a precarious nature is precisely the environment which can at the same time shake self-sufficiency and develop responsibility. Even here the personal-spiritual level must then, in the seventh place, be the key to our solution. What if there are accidents in nature, from our point of view? Are natural laws our final category of interpretation? Are not regularities and irregularities in the natural realm subject to the highest purpose that we see? We mean by that precisely that the irregularities have a function as well as the regularities. Nature is the right medium, with its constancy and inconstancy, with its predictability and unpredictability, to foster in us at the same time initiative, responsibility, and creative insight, and also common dependence on something be-

[7] *History of Dogma*, Vol. V, p. 204.

yond us all, the need to co-operate with each other, and a feeling of constant insecurity on the plane of human power, goodness, and wisdom.

It is good that we can plan; nature is that far stable. It is also good that we cannot plan except precariously; nature is that much uncertain. It is good that we can create, can invent. It is also good that the use of our creations and our inventions is precarious. We are not made to live here in perfect security and satisfaction. With us all power is precarious. Nature testifies to this and contributes to our higher purpose for being here. To dismiss the evidence for purpose simply because we have not accepted the highest purpose, indicated by the Cross, is to put our own selves athwart our chance of seeing. In Christ "all things cohere."[8] Rationality must be defined from the highest perspective of truth, not from the preconceptions of our own wants. Rationality is continuous only from God down, never from man up. Reason must become religious to become adequate. We are "renewed unto knowledge" when we see "after the image of him that created."[9] Instability in nature, in any case, including sudden death or slow death, death by natural catastrophe or by gradual decaying, is God's heavy hand on our will to self-sufficiency.

Stability in nature gives us the chance to plan, to grow, to become responsible, to develop initiative. Both are for our good. The final way of nature with us, in fact, death, our last enemy, the very core symbol of natural evil, is itself the ultimate and unavoidable frustration of our will to live by means of our own power. To us it seems altogether obvious that nature gives us the right chance for security and satisfaction and also the needed insecurity to make us at least begin in this life to seek for God and enough dissatisfaction with life as it is to make us long for the truer and fuller kinds of satisfaction. Accidents on our earth or in the stellar places can confidently be left in His hands who

[8] Colossians 1:17.
[9] *Ibid.*, 3:10.

made both the earth and those stellar places and who keeps them enough in their orbits to allow us all the life that we know, and a far better one even here, if we more fully trusted and obeyed him both personally and collectively.

Nature does indeed both give and take in such a way as to drive us human beings together. The technological pyramid that we have raised on nature, depending as it does upon a highly diversified division of labor, intensifies and widens this need for one another. There is much loose talk about industrialized man having no need of God, as the farmer and the sailor do. Our technological civilization has not yet been so entirely without all destruction, so entirely creative and co-operative, that by our conquest of nature we have done away with our need for God. The power that we possess is far from either foolproof or sinproof.

Perhaps we shall yet see that nature intensely cultivated makes us the more intensely dependent upon God. Perhaps we shall yet see that freedom from a wide, direct dependence upon nature is merely a freedom weighed the more heavily in the scales of God. The use of nature is still our trust that cannot be defied without remedial punishment. If nature were merely constant, without accident of weather or wind, without the obstacles of disease or sudden destruction, without "the curse" of toiling for our daily bread, without the collapse of mind and nerve, without the necessity, in short, for co-operation if we are to have human freedom and security, our rich, genuine fellowship, in the best sense that we know it, would be impossible.

Nor does nature suffer on the non-sentient level. Earthquakes do not suffer. Hurricanes do not suffer. Floods do not suffer. The surface of the earth, the pressures of the air currents, the locations of moisture are merely adjusted. The people who suffer can react to suffering either here or in God's bigger world. Natural destruction has no meaning except to those who can mean something with it, read meaning from it, or get meaning out of it.

Where there is meaning, moreover, there can be the understanding gradually of both means and ends.

There is a level in between, however, where there is experience of suffering, yet hardly any interpretation of it, even in whole-reaction, as far as we can judge. That is the realm of animal life. We are presently to discuss this realm and how to treat it. Brand Blanshard treats the perceptual level as "implicit inference,"[10] and the organism of bodies-in-nature as "a half-way house between inanimate matter and conscious mind."[11] Although animals do not have free ideas, or concepts employed in logical inference, they may, at certain high levels, have implicit whole-meanings. We just do not know. C. S. Lewis, besides, in *The Problem of Pain*, has moved the point of sentiency very high up into the organic realm—perhaps too high; but he has at least a real point in that low-grade experience must be basically different from ours, and in that the problem of pain in that world must in no way be treated from the perspective of intensive human sensitivity. Either the experience may be lower than we think and therefore there is less actual pain, incomparable to our experience; or else it may be higher than we think, in which case there may be the experience of incipient, implicit whole-meanings.

Before we go on to treat animal suffering, however, we must observe that the basic drive of nature is satisfaction. Life on the organic level affirms rather than denies itself by the very process of self-perpetuation. The instinctive reaction all through nature is self-preservation, the existential affirmation that life is good. Philosophers and pleasure seekers weary faster of life, in many cases, than those who struggle almost desperately with its problems in concrete ways. The rabbit chased by the fox accents with every skip and hop that life is good. The fish on the line switches and beats its affirmation that it is better to be alive than dead. Life contains much more pleasure than pain, more pleasure,

[10] *The Nature of Thought*, Vol. i, p. 96.
[11] *Ibid.*, p. 164.

satisfaction, and beauty than we may be able to understand. Human anxiety and sophistication dull the senses and the sense of sheer satisfaction in living. Those who have even occasionally got close to earth in its primitive power to move the depths of our being know that the poets of nature are too lyrical mostly for those who have no eyes to see, no ears to hear, no pulsing life to feel.

Although we cannot adequately grasp levels of life not our own, the basic thing about nature is, however, not continual destruction but continual creativity, interrupted and thwarted by destruction. Destruction cannot explain the origin and maintenance of nature, nor its order. Creative power must do that. Destruction is adjectival, a negative instance of a positive reality. Even animals live more with their own kinds in constructive activity than in destructive devouring. Co-operation is more characteristic of nature than conflict. The little fishes swim longer with their own kind than they dwell in the mouth of the big fish that gobbles them up. Some even grow up or there would be no big fish. The robin spends more time with its mate and with other birds than with the cat or the fox that eats it. It even lives to have young ones. Even though Joad may say that we underestimate pain in animal life and cite W. H. Hudson, a naturalist, to the effect that four-fifths of the birds die an unnatural death and live in states of fear from "slight disquiet" to "agonizing terror,"[12] the writer is convinced, as far as his own watching is concerned, that life is in the saddle rather than death, satisfaction rather than suffering, pleasure rather than pain. There are more well birds than sick ones. The time that they are not chased and hurt is longer than when they are. We say this seriously and with no intention to minimize our problem. It is so easy to exaggerate one way or the other that the temptation to do so is always at hand. Our perspective, however, must be as sane and as right as possible. Nature is not basically "red in tooth and claw." It is basically

[12] *God and Evil*, pp. 67-68.

creative, the womb of life rather than of death, of satisfaction rather than of suffering, of beauty rather than of ugliness.

We must admit freely, however, that we are up against real questions. The problem of animal pain is not the only problem about natural evil. We are not bothered about cosmic accidents or facts of that kind, if there are any. Yet why, for instance, did God start creating our cosmic epoch on so low a level of evolution? Why could He not have started right off with man? Why did He take so long to reach the Christian level of experience? Why did there have to be such low levels even of anthropoid life? Why have some evolutions gone wrong? Why have some species of life perished entirely? Are the satisfactions in animal life generally great enough to warrant its grievous suffering? Does that suffering lead somewhere or is it meaningless? Can the development of life in general on levels lower than self-consciousness justify individual suffering among animals?

Will each individual life ever created go on to its fuller purpose? Are there animal heavens in God's wider heaven? In the light of God's immeasurable difference from us and that life which shall be ours, are we a great distance from the animal world? Are not some animals farther along in their development than idiots or some babies that die? Can lower levels of life constitute an inclusive common being, some common life capable of general satisfaction and achievement? Is all life joined in the great ocean of God's being and is consciousness and individual being for all creatures but the temporarily isolated locus of the development of life in the ocean of God's being, the pooled reservoir of sufferings and satisfactions below adequate individuation, sufficient to account for, and justify, animal suffering? Life lives on life, serving life, thus serving itself, the suffering of one creature often being the satisfaction of some other creature. Is individuation at so low a level that common animal life is more important than the special instant? Surely nature develops too many instances for individual comfort in order to maintain and perpetuate the species.

Who shall solve this problem for us? How shall it be done? Surely what is true from the point of view of life in general may hardly be true from the point of view of the deer that runs before the hunter.

Most frankly we have no complete solution to offer. We wonder if the child notion of animal heavens is as childish as the sophisticated sneer of the denier. If pain is real, God must have a purpose with it or the highest claim of religion is palpably false. That purpose, too, must apply to every individual that experiences the pain. We can accept no less a solution. It seems less and less possible to us to explain animal pain on the basis of life in general. Even though the individual animal may not know that it has experienced pain, it nevertheless has. Nor can we be certain that each animal has so much more pleasure than pain that animal pain can be justified in that way. Pain often ends its experience and rounds off other experiences of suffering and fear. We have, for these reasons, come to feel that there is an evolution of each individual soul up to the level of self-consciousness, or at least human existence.

We in the West have much to learn from the East where this problem has been taken more seriously. Our higher level of grace, in many instances, has removed us farther from the level of creation. Are the roots of each human soul dug deep in the millennia of animal development? Are the lion and the rabbit, the snake and the mosquito, the horse and the wren actually in us, not in a general life stream, but individually, finding in us their fuller fruition and eventual individuation in a more permanent form? Or are we in some other realm to develop higher forms, maintaining individuality and basic memory, yet going imaginably far beyond earthly existence? There has been an evolution of body. Here we depend upon the animal world. Why can there not be an evolution of soul which is latent in the consciousness of God?

There need be no continuation of the body since that is of nature, of earth earthy, from dust to dust. Yet each life as a life may be indescribably precious to God and guided in its development from the lowest level of process to the highest. How fast the process as a whole has gone from the point of view of God, and this period of preparation, though long in our eyes, is not a sign of meaninglessness but of God's indescribably careful way of working. Then the disappearance of species in the process of evolution has no meaning. No life has been lost. All lives have been kept in the care of God and allowed to go on to such an appropriate form for it as God has prepared. How rich is not then our background? How close we must be to all of earth, to all of God's creatures. Not one sparrow is forgotten in the sight of God.[13]

In this way of looking at things we have not severed man from nature, nor have we merged him back into its lower levels. We have glorified and given meaning to nature all the way through and we have given man a place a little lower than the angels, as a matter of fact, as a child of God not only by creation but by adoption. The fact of evolution is too new for Christian theology to have come basically to grips with it. Our friends in the East in their deeper wrestling with these problems have led the way. God has not left Himself without a witness anywhere, and we have much to learn from the long and large prevalence of this way of looking at things.

The universal vicariousness of suffering, even on levels below its being understood, then also gets basic meaning. Life lives on life and by means of life. Up to the level of Christian self-sacrifice, or of self-sacrifice on any level from the bird mother for its young, the individual for the herd, the member for the tribe, the soldier for the country, the Christ for all humanity, there is mostly involuntary or ungrasped vicariousness. Life kills life. The tribe kills the human sacrifice for the good of the whole

[13] Cf. Luke 12:6.

tribe, the country drafts the soldier to kill and to be given for the country. The higher life goes, however, and the higher the spirit emerges, the more life can be freely and triumphantly given for life. Vicariousness becomes voluntary and meaningfully intended, often even against common pressures and social stigmas. Life must live in life and feed on life. The question is whether life shall be in the fellowship of self-giving love which does away finally with individual conflict or whether it shall be a devouring of life by life on the level of selfish conflict.[14] God Himself finally takes all earthly lives, devours them, for a new existence. He is the truth of creative co-operation and of endless life more abundant. Shall He not do right in the end in His way with every life that He has created?

All must lose their lives. At a certain point of our development we can lose our lives into the fuller meaningfulness of God's purpose and thus find them forever. God's creativity begins at the lowest levels but is destined for the highest end. Evolution may tell us our *background*, how God began to make us from the dust of the earth and through all the stages of His days of creation. The Gospel, however, must tell us our *foreground*, where we are going. Perhaps in future existences we may wonder even more at our having had to begin at so low a level as human life! Perhaps from that higher perspective our human development now and for vast periods to come may seem intolerably slow. Who knows what vast worlds of life, not confined to our kind of space and time, if at all, may even now surround our tiny history? Let him who knows speak up.

The whole problem of the animal world is, in any case, a secondary problem of knowledge. It is not a central problem of faith. It cannot determine our ultimate perspective. Suffering is part of all life. Pain is a teacher and fear is a guide in human as well as in animal life. Life hangs together. We must know life

---

[14] Is not Christian pacifism, then, God's fullest realization of fellowship, as far as it is genuine, so far?

through our kind of experience. We can know it in no other way dependably and adequately. Our suggestions toward a solution of suffering in the animal world are consequently not on the level with the rest of our interpretation. They must necessarily be more speculative, more part-thinking. Yet we believe that God is more sensitive than we are to the pain of the least of His creatures, that not a sparrow falleth without His knowing and participating in it, directly or indirectly, and that He who is Agape has His adequate way of dealing with this problem far better and more fully than we can know or think. From the point of view of knowledge, thus, we may believe that God works with animals fulfilling their lives not only justly but creatively and redemptively *in some such way* as we have suggested.

The whole problem, however, is subsumptive; since it is only speculative it can be viewed only from a partial perspective. The nature of process, its origin, and its end cannot be explained on the level of animal life. That is not our highest level of truth, our ultimate existential perspective. Nor is animal life a static fact eternally. A cosmic second ago there was no animal life. A fraction of a cosmic second ago there was no human life. A fraction of that ago there was no recorded history. He who has thrust this whole process, this whole fact of animal and human life, so suddenly upon the screen on the larger purpose has His dynamic and fulfilling way to deal with this level of life. There is on it no fact that can hinder us from identifying assuredly the most high and the most real. That problem, too, is our most difficult. Yet it pales in the brilliance of "the glory of his grace."[15]

The more we see the push of Purpose in process in its own perspective the more we are amazed at how incommensurately greater are the goodness and the power of God than any and all aspects of evil in process. Existentially, this problem pales in proportion to the intensification of the full faith. The more we look at what is central in truth and the less we are lost in what is peripheral,

[15] Ephesians 1:6.

the more we find illumined even what is peripheral. The foundations of truth are strong and solid. Though reason cannot fully bridge the gap between the most good and the most real, not only because the evidence is not yet in but also because there are realms of experience which are not fully accessible to our knowledge, yet the evidence from the explanations of the beginnings of process, its end, and its present intellectual and practical problems is forcefully cumulative. The faith that has been illumined and empowered by the most high can meet in calm confidence and much seeing even the problems of the most low.

We can also say, to return to more positive grounds, that nature with its semi-independence of both God and man constitutes the necessary medium whereby God can lead man generally without forcing him specifically. If there were no nature, if nature were simply the direct organization of God's consciousness, if there were no created realm in a real sense, if all our dealings were directly with God, we should have either to obey Him directly or to rebel directly against His will. We should have either a complete determinism or else a freedom strong enough to rebel permanently against God. Our rebellion would not be that of men touched with ignorance and weakness, dragged down by the claims of the flesh, but would rather be spirit straight against Spirit. The best, the true, and the right could not then be learned by the trying for oneself in an experimental situation. Things would be either black or white. Growth would not be indirect and individuating. Most troubles with respect to the relation between freedom and determinism arise from an abstract, logical contrasting of two entities, God and man, which never exist in actuality without a third, nature, whereby the whole relation is shifted from the direct to the indirect, at least as a large and immensely important aspect of the relation.

By creating man in His own image, by putting him with certain capacities and inclinations in a certain kind of environment, God conditions and controls him without directly determining him.

Unless He would thus lead him by both His severity and His goodness through the channels of experience in nature and history in order to have him see and find for himself what the nature of his own true good really is, man would be pretty much of an automaton. Nature with its precariousness and destructiveness is this medium, this school, this training ground, whereby God makes the prodigal hungry that he might bethink himself, repent of his ways, and come to himself, to remember his home, and more than before to understand not only his father's bounty but his wonderful goodness. If the son is to stay at home with full understanding and appreciation, he must at least have had the option of the faraway land. If the son does not come home by means of the hunger and discomfort of our nature in this cosmic epoch, the death of nature in us, or our severance from nature at the end, namely death, shocks us into considering the place where we are and where we are going. What will happen then we do not know except that we shall be alone with the Alone without all external lean-tos, with no hiding place and with no external bases for self-security. Natural "evil" thus has an indispensable function in the wisdom of God. Thus in God's time, the intermediate steps of life in nature make way for the immediate, for will against Will, deed against judgment, and for God's fuller way with us in a new realm prepared for us by His wisdom.

CHAPTER VIII

Means and Ends

Does this not mean that we believe, however, that the ends justify the means? Is not God in any case using evil means? How, then, can He be perfectly good? We believe, rather, that means can be judged truly only by relation to the ends. A painful surgical operation which is necessary to restore to health a damaged life threatened by destruction is good as a means. The means must be judged by the best way available according to the nature of things to accomplish a worthy end. Yet means are good as means, and not as ends. Good means may be very bad ends. The Cross, for instance, that greatest goodness treated badly unto death, is good as a means but not as an end. The Crown of Christian fellowship effected by it must ever entwine about and over it. The Crown would not be what it is except in terms of the Cross. That Crown without the Cross would not be *that* Crown.

Christian fellowship can be had at no other price than victorious suffering. "Without shedding of blood is no remission" of sin.[1] Vicarious suffering is the tap root of Christian fellowship. We shy away from the means, but the end is because of the means. Our self-sufficiency must be broken through and our sufficiency in God with one another where all the members have "the same care one for another"[2] must be established. It is simply useless specula-

[1] Hebrews 9:22.
[2] I Corinthians 12:25.

tion to set up our highest ends, a mature fellowship of love, for instance, and then demand that the end be also the means to effect it, or that it be effected without the necessary means. The green fruit is good as a stage but not as an end. Yet growth requires the green fruit before the ripe, the blade before the corn in the ear.

All talk of means and ends that is not rooted solidly in the selective actual which is our standard of truth, in God's action and meaning in Jesus Christ, is wind and weather. Given the purpose of the process, the meaning of existence, we must judge the means to it solely in terms of their capacity or appropriateness to effect the dominant end, purpose, or meaning. Are nature and history, for instance, suitable means to effect, or at least to begin to effect, a God-centered fellowship? Such questions and such questions alone are legitimate in the light of the highest truth that we know, based not only on the end of process but also on the explanation of its origin and origins and upon the practical requirements of our deepest needs in the present stage of process. Truth must organically combine what was in the beginning, now is, and ever shall be, the eternal behind the temporal, suggesting the fullest understanding of all the stages of time.

In the end the discussion of means must be in terms of cosmic purpose and effectiveness. The question comes down to whether or not God is justified in using these means—experience, history, suffering, the Cross, death—to effect His end. We must not speak abstractly, mixing our perspectives or starting from too narrow perspectives that cannot fulfill the total functions of truth. We must not speak irresponsibly as though no means ought to be used at all, or as though the means ought to be as perfected to begin with as the ends. Personal development means growth. A Gospel of grace, of forgiveness, of the fruits of the Spirit presupposes sin, suffering, and redemption. A Gospel of willing, understanding family fellowship requires that the sons think and try for themselves their ways until they know and accept in love and joy the full nature of the family fellowship.

Does this not limit God, however, to the compossible, to what things are possible together? Is not the perspective of the compossible, after all, the perspective of the limitations imposed by the nature of our kind of experience, by our kind of history, by our kind of cosmic epoch? The compossible must, indeed, be defined in terms of the highest truth that we know. All other approaches to the problem are up in the air. We know God's nature in terms of the highest instance of it in history, which also best explains the process as a whole, now, past, and to be. The compossible must then be defined in terms of God's nature and purpose for concrete lives within our actual situation, not by logical abstractions, springing from abstract or partial perspectives, like total pleasure.[3]

To express one's own nature perfectly, Agape, by providing the perfect conditions for the sharing of one's life in a fellowship of growing in grace and creativity is no limitation. Limitations are restrictions or thwartings imposed from within or without which are contrary to one's nature and purpose. Naturally there are things contrary to God's will in history. Look at His will and then compare it with history! Yet that history be as a means is not contrary to His purpose according to our highest perspective of solid or real knowledge. History is a means, not an end, and must be judged as such. Within it is the partial and anticipatory realization of ends, and the struggle is ever between realization and realizability, the former lagging far behind the latter. Yet God is sufficient in love, wisdom, and power to condition and to control perfectly for "the final unity and fitness of things"[4] the total process of which we see only the smallest bit, and that in broken form, within this history of ours.

That there be a free finding of His will by our making mistakes and even by our rebelling against His will, for the sake of deepening fellowship through mistakes and sin, but also through learn-

[3] Cf. Deane, *St. Anselm,* p. 205.
[4] Origen, "De Principiis," *Ante-Nicene Fathers,* Vol. IV, p. 261.

ing and forgiveness, and for the sake of the deepening at the same time of each individual, for the sake, perhaps, of learning eternally the Father's heart more fully even after the process of our kind of mistakes and our sins is over—that there be this free finding and the kind of world necessary to it is not a limitation of God's will. This very situation is, rather, the historic expression of His will. Even to call this compossible "self-limitation" is to define infinity from the perspective of power rather than from the perspective of Agape. God's sovereignty in Agape is not curtailed but expressed in the creation of this kind of world as a means. His limitation of power in order to allow human freedom is in reality His free and humble sharing of His power for our sake, and thus not a limitation of Himself but His gracious giving of Himself according to His infinite will.

God sees that the world is good as a means even as He made it. He created this world to be the earth, not to be the final heaven. The whole creation must go from the garden of innocence, natural amoralism, through a cursed nature and history, with a Cross at the center of it, which leads onward through long ages of wanderings in the world, often in the wilderness of disobedience and the consequences of sin, far away from the original garden, until we reach the better garden of fulfilling Christian fellowship where God walks *wanted* in the garden.

But God, by the ineffable skill of His wisdom, transforming and restoring all things, in whatever manner they are made, to some useful aim, and to the common advantage of all, recalls those very creatures which differed so much from each other in mental conformation to one agreement of labor and purpose; so that, although they are under the influence of different motives, they nevertheless complete the fulness and perfection of one world, and the very variety of minds tends to one end of perfection. For it is one power which grasps and holds together all the diversity of the world, and leads the different movements towards one work, lest so immense an undertaking as that of the world should be dissolved by the dissensions of souls.[5]

What seems, then, the self-limitation of God's freedom, or His limitation to the compossible, is simply the expression of His freedom in His basic nature and purpose, namely, to share His freedom with sons of His creation. It is the full using of His freedom that He might share it with willing sons who know His goodness and who share understandingly His eternal joy and being. God cannot, then, be considered limited by the compossible. The compossible is rather defined by God's action and meaning in history. "In His operation God is revealed to us."[6] That God's children start as such and not as full-grown adults and that the conditions of the home be appropriate to the rearing of children is not the limitation of God's nature and will, but rather the historic expression for them.

[5] *Ibid.*, p. 268.
[6] Barth, *The Doctrine of the Word of God*, p. 426.

CHAPTER IX

God and Suffering

But is this stress on God's eternal joy, which He wants to share, itself justified? If God is love and the world is evil, must He not suffer with it? How, then, can He have joy to share? If, moreover, God is eternally creating, must He not suffer always? Must He not, in that case, always have *some* creation with which to suffer? This second question, for a fuller answer, must await the analysis of the relation of history to eternity. Can heaven, in any case, be the perfectly satisfactory fellowship which is taken by us to be the goal of God's grace, if God must suffer while He keeps creating? Does not hedonism have legitimately the partial power to ask that question?

The Cross has its deepest meaning as God's work for man, according to our theme of God's work in history, as God takes into His own life our own sufferings in order to deliver us from sin, and eventually for a state finally beyond suffering. Can God both suffer with us and be at the same time basically blissful? The positive, of course, is primary. The Creator shares His joy. Agape is greater than grace, God's being in Himself greater than His relation to us, eternity greater than history. The travails of creation, moreover, are mostly the growing pains and the emotional adjustments and maturing, including the tantrums and the stubborn sets, against the parents, of God's children. The fact is that God's being and beauty, God's bliss and glory, are entirely incommensurate with our measure of being and knowing. If the sufferings in nature affect Him, whether directly or indirectly, God is incommensurately, incomparably less hurt than a robust athlete would be if He put his thigh between a slowly falling pebble and an infant's face, or between a falling twig and a crawling ant.

Yet these illustrations fail to signify the qualitative and immense difference between God's full glory and our sufferings, "which are for a moment." A mother's dismay at hearing the infant cry at her taking away something the infant had seized and should not have, might suggest something. The mother is sorry with the infant only because the infant does not know better. God knows and cares about His infants' troubles, but His purposes and joy are so steadfast and beyond doubt, He so knows and rejoices in the end of the process, in the sharing of His creative joy, that His sympathy does not dampen or detract from His intrinsic glory and overflowing well-being. This sympathy out of perfect strength is, rather, a part and sign of His glory. A mother holding in her arms a child who has been desperately ill and who is now fast recovering can both sympathize with the child's moans and yet overflow with joy.

The nature of God's suffering is a topic almost certainly beyond our comprehension. What can it possibly mean? God has no suffering from an imperfect wisdom, from a doubtful mind, from defensive fear, from anxiety, from a sense of insecurity. God's suffering is completely outgoing, through and through redemptive. It is pure sympathy, the feeling with the creatures, His own children, a craving for them the fuller fellowship. Jesus endured the Cross "for the joy that was set before him."[1] Perhaps the joy was not only after the event. Is there not a joy beyond ordinary experience precisely in redemptive suffering? Have we taken on the suffering of the world even in the least measure without feeling an overwhelming joy which can never be matched by any

[1] Hebrews 12:2.

other experience that we have had? There may be no joy so great and no peace so deep in history as truly unselfish suffering when it is authentically redemptive and truly for the fellowship which springs from these deep sources of common experience one for the other. God's cross may then be real in sympathy and in suffering, and yet not thwart but rather deepen and enrich His joy. We can throw our burdens on Him, for He understands. He carries all sorrows and shares all sufferings. God knows, cares, and suffers with us.

Yet God suffers *in history*. The eternal Father is basically bliss, the glory which shares His being through process as it becomes fulfilled. That is the reason that the doctrine of compassion, or co-passion, namely, the Father suffering with the Son, has been declared heretical. God suffers as a Son but not as the Father. What that most deeply stands for is that, although the suffering of God is real in history, it is nevertheless only temporary and incidental; the joy of God is fully real, whole-life, and eternal. The fact that God suffered and suffers as Son alone, on Calvary, and each day, as the saints fulfill the sufferings of Christ, stands for the truth that the Cross is a means, the deepest and best means, to the highest possible end. The means is temporary while the end is final and permanent. There is basic joy in God, basic glory; besides, there is also the joy of suffering for us, taking up our burdens gladly to carry them for us on His strong back; beyond this, there is consummately the joy of a perfectly assured anticipation—when the fellowship of suffering turns into the fellowship of gratitude, co-operation, and free creativity. God's suffering in history is as deep and real as all human misery, all misery of any kind. Yet immeasurably greater is the ocean of His joy. The end is incomparably greater than the means. The final perspective, however, is *neither suffering nor joy*, but the reality of the eventually effective fellowship.

God, moreover, does not create us for His own glory. He does not use suffering as a means to produce a fellowship for His own satisfaction, in any selfish sense. He rather overflows with joy in the sharing of His being. He gives to us. He creates for our sake. His nature is completely outgoing. He consequently identifies Himself with the sufferings of His children as they grow. He feels our sufferings in us. How much He can suffer beyond that is hard to understand, because all within His full purpose is for the best. He is fully opposed to sin as an end, inasmuch as rebellion against Him keeps us from sharing His bliss, but He wants us to find for ourselves what that bliss is. He must accordingly suffer in us even as we are kept from His joy by our evil acts or by our ignorance; He must also suffer in others as we hurt them. He shares our sorrows because He loves us and they are ours. Yet He knows why they are, and lives already in the full anticipation of the joy that shall be ours, which is so great that the suffering which is but for a moment is not worthy even to be compared with it. In His eternity of joy our history of suffering is but a drop. He knows the ocean of His glory which awaits us.

When we sin, we hurt ourselves and others, and God in ourselves and in others. This suffering, however, does not detract from the primary joy of His being, from His perfect purpose. God's joy includes His redemptive activity. Jesus may falter on the Cross, being in that respect human; but not God. We must see this problem in the fullest possible perspective of God, not in our own small corner. Even while God shares our sorrows on our level, in us, He yet overflows eternally with joy, saying: "Have faith, have peace, have joy." Jesus gives His peace on the way to the Cross, a peace so deep that the world can neither give it nor take it away.

The trouble with much Christian faith is that it has lost its radiance. It is not centered in God's promises. It takes the troubles of the world more seriously than God's glory, which He longs to give to the world in order thereby to solve its problems. We Christians lack faith. We sing of the Cross; we should, indeed; but the Cross must be seen in the full triumph of the Resurrection.

That is the heart of the Gospel; God's conquering love is the good news from God. He has "despoiled the principalities," made "a show of them openly, triumphing over them."[2] We can help the world more than in any other way when we find the real "joy and peace in believing" because we "abound in hope, in the power of the Holy Spirit."[3]

People are full of fears. They need faith. They need faith in God, who loves them completely, that they might find their full security and creative freedom in Him. They cannot, furthermore, believe words about faith. Faith must be shown. Children imitate those who are genuinely happy. They want to know and to share their secret. The secret is to take up the Cross daily to follow the Christ. A Church that dares to renounce the standards, attitudes, and ways of the world to live wholly, by the grace of God, for it, a Church that will share the world's sufferings as its own, will find joy both now in the fellowship of redemptive suffering and eventually in the ensuing heavenly fellowship.

The fellowship of believers must be the fellowship triumphant. Lukewarm Christians have not tasted the real wine of the Spirit, the overflowing joy which under all circumstances can be had when we truly live according to the law of the Spirit which *is* joy and peace. Such joy is like God's and is the best testimony to His presence in us and in the Christian fellowship as a whole. Even if God does create eternally—and what that means the writer cannot think, for serial thinking exhausts itself in unfathomable eternity—even such sharing of the suffering on the part of His children who are yet growing up does not spoil either God's joy or that of the grown family. It is, rather, part of that deeper creative and redemptive joy of triumphant fellowship. We must not reduce the primary situation to the temporary conditions, attitudes, and points of view of the means. Especially falsifying is the perspective of God's unwilling children who resent being

[2] Colossians 2:15.
[3] Romans 15:13.

severally members of the body, who want their own pleasure in their own way. We must learn to look at the whole picture from the point of view of truth, from the point of view of God's eternal love sharing itself, at least from the point of view of "the body . . . building up of itself in love."[4]

Yet the problem will not down. From the hedonistic premise that all ought to be altogether and ever pleasant, that there should be no pain or sorrow at all or ever, there is simply no solution either for the origin or for the end of evil. If God creates eternally (as we shall see, the problem must be put beyond the inverted parentheses of historical knowledge, beyond the limits of faith even as our highest and fullest synthesis of faith and reason), there will always be some cross in God's heart. Then suffering must ever be an aspect of eternity. Then the end is always accompanied by some means. We suspect that our difficulty is due to equating time and eternity qualitatively. We tend to put the Father on the Cross. Does the fact that God suffers in history stand only for the truth that historic problems have no intrinsic relevance for eternity while eternity nevertheless has full relevance for our historic problems? Are the relations between the eternal and the temporal, as far as the relativities are concerned, one-way? Are we not requiring that God need the world in the same way that the world needs God? Are only the positive relations between time and eternity real, the negative being non-being, potent in time, but powerless in eternity? Yet if we make this distinction do we not deny the immanence which is characteristic of theism? Have we not gone a good way toward deism?

Are we not also denying the basic truth of Christianity that Agape descends to our level of sin, ignorance, and misery to operate there? Or can it operate there in its perfect purity being perfectly transcendent in quality in the sense that it ever keeps its nature and perspective complete, never entering ours, while yet being always there for us to enter? May God come down *to* and *for*

[4] Ephesians 4:16.

the sinner but never truly *with* the sinner? He is with the child
of His creation, but not with him as a rebel. He is against the rebel
even while for the child. Is not that the case? God is with His
person, His child, His image, His own spirit in created humility
and concealment, but not with sin, not with any imperfection in
the sense of union or appropriation.

God is thus truly here to and for us as we are, but only truly
with us as we are in Him or accept Him. God never identifies
Himself except with truth and grace. Is this a solution of fellowship on the basis both of sin and of holiness and of suffering as
well? Then God's suffering is in and through those who accept His
love in history and works through them, but the saints, too, are
then to and for the sinful world as they, the saints, are in the
spirit, in eternity, and with the sinful, relative, and suffering world
as they, the saints, actually are. We suspect that some such solution there must be, or else at this point we strike a paradox which
partially prevents the full synthesis of whole-reason and whole-
response. Faith, then, must go beyond our fullest seeing. We must
not, of course, court mystery as an escape from right whole-thinking. Nor must we escape right whole-thinking by refusing to see
mystery where it truly is. We must not try to evade the intrinsic
limitations of our perspectives as creatures. On this point we are
still considerably baffled.

The question of God's eternal creativity is not simple. Agape is
outgoing concern for fellowship. This we know concretely in terms
of our highest decisive instance of God's action and meaning in
the life of Jesus Christ. Yet our knowledge is from this highest
instance *concretely*, not from its general meaning *abstractly*. Thus
we must not say that God is always creating as though He needed
something. God, as Plato suggests in the "Timaeus," creates not
from need, or "jealousy,"[5] but from overflowing strength. This
overflowing is not a need, not a lack, but a spontaneous act. It is
on the personal, not on the natural or on the impersonal, level.

[5] In *The Dialogues of Plato*, Jowett trans. Vol. III, p. 450.

God's love is not like the rays of the sun shining equally everywhere. It is not a force like gravitation. God is no unmoved Mover, like Aristotle's God. Therefore we *cannot* even say serially that he has created more worlds than this. Serial thinking always gets back to zero sometime; and the problem of creation is no more solved in eternity than when we think God created this world only. The writer cannot conceive of an infinite series without a beginning. He can rest satisfied with neither infinite regression nor infinite repetition. Infinite regression, for him, is just an evasion of the problem. If there is addition, if the new is genuinely new, there must also be subtraction. A continually expanding infinity that always is all, yet becomes more, seems to him to lead back to the eternally self-existent, but also at some time to a *first* creation. In that case, we are still left with the problems of special creation, of this creation. Infinite cycles and eternal repetition, furthermore, deny the reality of the new that is our very basis for knowledge. Eternal creation is an abstraction not required by our reflexive superspective except negatively as the denial of the adequacy for the existential ultimate of our perspective of present process.

Origen has well put the case for God's eternal activity:

> And who that is capable of entertaining reverential thoughts or feelings regarding God, can suppose or believe that God the Father ever existed, even for a moment of time, without having generated this Wisdom? For in that case he must say that either God was unable to generate wisdom before he produced her, so that he afterwards called into being her who formerly did not exist, or that He possesses the power indeed, but—what cannot be said of God without impiety—was unwilling to use it; both of which suppositions, it is patent to all, are alike absurd and impious.[6]

This, if applied to creation, is falsely to universalize the creative activity of God, either putting it on less than a personal plane or

[6] *Op. cit.*, p. 246.

motivating the personal act by need, whether in terms of outer or inner lack.

We must, first of all, not eternalize the problems of process. Then, secondly, we must not universalize God's activity in our process. All that we can legitimately universalize and eternalize is his own Agape, who is self-existent. His outgoing concern may be eternally within the perfect divine society, symbolized by the Trinity, within His uncreated being. It may be for His "wisdom," an eternal generation of the Son. It must not be assumed in kind, direction, and problem to be like our creation. That is falsely to define God in terms of our creation rather than creation "by means of a consideration of God."[7] The whole line of reasoning is, however, falsely speculative as soon as inference from our basis of truth, the pointing of process, becomes more important or true than the basis from which it itself necessarily proceeds.

Special creation, in any case, is the immediate fact, the concrete basis of knowledge. Creation is a concept, pointing process is a fact, that leads beyond itself to the fuller perspectives of the reflexive superspective. After years of struggle with this question the writer has become convinced that we are creatures of process, of our kind of time, of the created content of time, and that we cannot take the point of view ultimately of God's eternity. If someone can show him how he can solve the relation between time and eternity, between being and becoming, that will affirm, not deny, the basic facts of pointing process and the fulfillment of the Christian fellowship in God, or produce any metaphysics that will be true, with respect to both validity and adequacy, he will be forthright in admitting, whether with joy or with sorrow, that the problem has a real solution. Subjective definitions of time that evade the ultimate issues, reducing them to aspects of human experience, simply will not do. Existential thinking that denies the reality of the problem except to immediate decisions cannot satisfy.

[7] Cf. Przywara, *Polarity*, p. 86.

As far as we can see, then, it is not evasion or flight from reason to maintain that history is a parenthesis within eternity. God lives and sees on both sides. We see only bit by bit within them. A Japanese student has quoted a Japanese professor to the writer as saying that the parentheses must be turned around so as to point out in this fashion) (. We stand between the backs, so to speak, of the parentheses of time. Aulén stresses that honest thinking must recognize "the limits of our faith."[8] Within the parentheses is the true stuff of eternity, but only selectively actual. The main bulk of our history is not of the nature of God's eternal being and purpose. It is more means than ends. When we see more fully we shall surely know how distorted and perverted our vision was and how beggarly small was our highest and truest thought.

The basic paradox in all thinking lies between God's eternity and man's time, between infinite being and finite becoming. To rationalize this away is to lose the dimension of depth, to lose the transcendence, too, that shifts the perspective from man's knowledge to God's power, wisdom, and love, from human reason to divinely sustained faith.

This, then, is the answer in part, added to what we already have said about the joy of redemptive suffering and the incommensurate nature between God's and man's experience of suffering; God does not create from need, making immaturity as a constant part of God's family perpetually necessary, and in the long last, anyway, we cannot penetrate beyond the backs of the parentheses of history to explain the experience of God as though He were a case in human psychology. Though we must serve the Lord with all our mind, we hardly serve Him most fully by reducing the infinite to one of us.

How much an ant thinks is questionable; yet surely an ant can far better, immeasurably better, understand Abraham Lincoln than we can God *in all His fullness of being*. Even such a comparison seems presumptuous in that the lower finite can indubitably

[8] *Den allmänneliga kristna tron*, p. 206.

interpret the higher finite better than the finite the infinite. We are given the privilege of being children of God to think, to know, and to love. Yet at this stage, however truly we may know God's love or, rather, be known by it, the fullness of that love both qualitatively and quantitatively is farther beyond us than heaven is beyond earth. "Eye has not seen, nor ear heard." "It doth not yet appear." If we are to establish our perspective truthfully this recognition must be a basic fact.

On this total question of whether or not the most high can also be the most real in view of the fact that if God is love He must suffer with His creatures and where there is suffering there is less than perfect joy, we have thus many answers. They are, nevertheless, of a tentative nature. We hope to ponder them more fully in connection with the doctrine of God. The first answer is to the effect that creation is not out of need but out of love's overflowing joy and strength. Creation need not always, therefore, have to be going on, as though God were a mechanism. He might live forever complete within the fellowship of His own divine society, symbolized by the Trinity. Suffering may thus be a temporary experience freely undertaken at one time for the sake of the fuller sharing of His fellowship. It need not be forever. There can be a final victory.

That there be suffering and love's sorrow in the effecting of the fellowship is part of the authentic compossible defined by God's nature, and when the hedonistic premise is removed as an ultimate standard, this is for the very best that there can be. In that case whole-response and whole-thinking go together. Our problem with this point of view is that it seems arbitrary to have God satisfied for eternity and then for some reason, or for no reason, create this epoch. The same problem besets any number of epochs if time did ever begin and will ever end, in a created sense. Then, again, if eternity has always been, why should not all possibilities for something new have been always exhausted? Eternal recurrence answers no real problem as to why the now is the now, why this creation is, this process of ours, which is the very basis of our knowledge.

The second possibility is that God keeps creating ever (think that who can!), suffering with His creations, but His suffering is merely an enriching aspect of His full fellowship life. His love shares itself always and always. His love is basically His joy, His wondrous fellowship, beyond human imagination, beyond all experience, waiting to be better and better known in ages to come. Yet that very love is never without the suffering of a historic cross. God's experience and ours in eternity will never be without redemptive activity. We shall always have depth and height and joy and riches of experience beyond thought and imaginative anticipation. Yet we shall never be free from being at the same time ministering spirits who find more joy in one soul in history that repents than in the ninety and nine that need no repentance. That suffering will be pure love without the anxieties of sin or the flesh.

The purity of its joy, of its self-giving, we cannot now understand. The fellowship of God's family, not absence of suffering, will be our highest joy. The Cross will not be exchanged for a Crown. The Crown will always be around the Cross, yet always above it, crowning it. We have no trouble with this point of view except for a lingering reluctance, perhaps of the man that is earthly, to accept suffering as a heavenly condition. There shall be no pain in heaven.[9] Shall this not also apply to the heart? Will not God wipe away every kind of tear from our eyes? Yet if God ever suffers, does He not suffer always? And if He suffers, shall not His children share their Father's lot? Can they be happy, if they love Him fully, knowing that He suffers? Can we, that is, then know the perfect joy of fellowship, the *whole-joy*, which includes suffering? Is this history, moreover, not exemplary rather than exceptional with regard to God's being and activity? Or does the Cross pertain to our history only? Then why was it compos-

[9] Cf. Revelation 21:4.

sible? Yet, at the same time, when all is said and done we must remember that the basic evidence is in a process that points. The superspective is our standard, not the problems of process. Has not also hedonism a partial power as a perspective: the right to bar means being ends, the cross being the crown, there being suffering in *heaven*?

The third possibility is that this problem is not for us to solve, but rather to surrender into God's hand. The attempt to solve it may be exactly what some earnest Christians call the sin of speculation. Is it not enough to know that sin can be forgiven, evil overcome, darkness put out? Process is pointing toward its solution. The Cross is the key to the effecting of the fellowship which we most deeply crave and which makes existence a blessing through and through. Why should we take the standpoint of eternity which only God can occupy? Is this not a sign of human vanity? Is this not precisely the eating of the fruit that banishes us from the garden of life and light? Is this not wanting to be like God in power and understanding?

The problem at least *seems* insoluble. We want to put it beyond the inverted parentheses of history. We think the problem belongs beyond the limits of faith. Yet we believe also that God wants us to love Him with all our minds. We believe that He wants understanding and willing children. We believe that He wants us to trust Him enough not to fear any taboo, so long as we love him and seek to serve him. The reason that we are so insistent in trying to deal with it is, in fact, that we want to see how far whole-response can also be whole-thinking. We cannot solve it fully. Yet we know also that a finite God cannot fully explain our basic problems. We see, therefore, as far as we can, in grace and truth, and leave the rest to the highest we have seen in history, the selective actual, which far transcends history as a whole.

If there is to be a solution, it may be that love suffers in history only. That is the classic solution of Christian theology. The modern world has taken to the idea of a suffering God. It has failed to distinguish between the Father and the Son. It forgets that the Son comes down to bear the Cross *in history*. The idea that the Father suffers with the Son is a heresy. Modern scholars have often dismissed this notion of heresy as un-Christian, due, in fact, to the idea of Greek philosophy that the perfect cannot suffer. Yet it may be that the early Fathers went far deeper than we. On this point Christian thought and Greek philosophy may both be right.

Royce, in modern times, has restated, for instance in *The World and the Individual*, the idea that evil is in time only. Eternity knows no frustration. Evil is basically the temporary frustration of the eternal good of God, *which has meaning to the frustration by the frustration,* but not to Him who lives in the perfection both of perfect being and of anticipated attainment. Eternal love then comes down in power and triumph to be in, with, and for all and any insofar as He comes to His own, lighting every man that comes into the world, *insofar* as he will and is in a position to receive Him. When that love becomes incarnated in history, it is within imperfect human forms which suffer—suffer from division within, suffer from imperfect surrender to God, suffer from the infirmities of the flesh, suffer from the darkness without that tries to put it out in order to defend itself. God is thus with His image, with His child, with the person, but He never becomes degraded to human sin, infirmities, or suffering. In His eternity he knows no division, no defeat, only triumphant sharing, irresistible sharing of His love.

Refusals of freedom and frustrations are of time, not of eternity. The Father hangs not on the Cross, but he who learned obedience through his suffering, who was made perfect through his sufferings, who suffered being tempted, who was compassed about with infirmities. The Saviour in glory is God. The Saviour in humility is Christ. As the love of God triumphs in a historic creature his sufferings with relation to God cease, his sufferings from temptations from within cease, yet his sufferings from the flesh and from others remain. They can be ended only by the cessation of historic existence.

Then suffering, too, ceases, and we join in God's fuller joy insofar as we have been perfected by His grace. God is with Jesus on the Cross; in victory, order, power, and peace; not in defeat, confusion, weakness and despair. They are of the human soul and flesh. God is ever close to us—but only as we open up to Him in faith, confidence, and joy. Even the pains of redemptive sufferings for a Christian must be a joy unspeakable and full of glory. Is it part of our weakness that we want God to share our weakness? Should He share our frustrations, the evils of process? Is this the reason why we must have a saviour in history, must have God's love incarnated; as H. Wheeler Robinson repeatedly stresses, "*actualized*" in history? We see in this question of God's suffering love basic problems but no definite obstacle to the identification of whole-response with whole-thinking, provided we remember that faith always flies off into heaven, seeking God's thoughts and ways beyond our own, that faith cannot be limited to our seeing, though it wants to see as truly and as far as it can, in order to worship God with all our mind within our whole surrendered self.

CHAPTER X

Evil and History

When the meaning of our existence is made clear, namely, that we are to pass from a needed attempt at self-security through self-despair to God-security, the meaning of history is also illumined. This is the seventh main area of application of the personal-spiritual level of interpretation. Man craves both freedom and fellowship, both freedom and security, both security and creative risk. History both drives and draws men to fellowship. Men are driven by their needs and fears. For food and shelter in a world like this men have had to co-operate. Co-operation has been a matter of physical situation as well as of drive for fellowship from within. Man's historic life has been not determined, but basically conditioned, by his economic needs. Marx saw a truth which, even if it cannot be made central to the interpretation of history, cannot be ignored. Property, tools, trade have driven men together by their needs and the feeling of insecurity in nature. The technological developments of the last three thousand years have altered the content of man's consciousness as he passed into a creature with world interests and world fears. International communication, trade and competition, greed and pride, national insecurities and identification of leaders with national loyalties over against the common welfare of man have brought men together whether for weal or woe, for simply larger interests or destructive warfare.

The external relations, at least, their material interests, and also

EVIL AND HISTORY89

their consciousness of one another, whether in hate, fear, or growing understanding and co-operation, have been enlarged with whirring speed. Telescope and microscope have enlarged man's vision. He has passed from chemical energy to the electric; from there to atomic or solar energy. Soon television may break down barriers of space and seeing, in climactic ways. Fear and need still drive men together according to permanent basic conditions. Man lives in a precarious environment with basically insecure spirit. All of man's history, on the physical side, witnesses to a gradual driving together of men for fellowship and security in virtue of both man's inner spirit and his outer situation. Yet alongside this external togetherness due to fear and need is the constant fight for freedom by individuals and groups; indeed, this constitutes one whole aspect of man's historic life.[1]

On this physical level is also the biological need to reproduce one's kind. The family, under whatever arrangement—and complete promiscuity has never been a social institution, only the danger sign of social disintegration[2]—is the intensification in intimate relations of this dual need for freedom and fellowship, for independence and security, for being oneself and yet being also part of a larger whole, being "a belonging" to a group. Here, too, man often wants to possess without yielding himself, being driven by his needs far beyond his being drawn by his loves. He wants to belong without being a belonging. He wants the sense of security without the responsibilities of full freedom. He wants to write the law of the fellowship rather than to be under the law. Few, indeed, there are who can live completely above the laws of duty.

Much trouble in general family relations stems from sentimentality. We romanticize marriage as though it were not largely

[1] For a fuller discussion of this topic cf. the writer's *The Christian Faith,* Chapter 3.
[2] Cf. E. O. James, *The Social Function of Religion,* Chapter 5, "Marriage and the Family," and the authorities he cites on this subject.

a selfish desire, the yielding to the deep drives within us. We often talk and act as though marriage were a matter of Agape, when most people have never known what it means to yield their whole selves to any other being, either human or divine. Luther is profound in his conception of such situations as vocations, where the very position we are in makes for, or holds us to, social relations beyond our actual wish. These situations, vocations like the family, curb our basic selfishness as natural men, inviting us and driving us to think and act beyond our small selves. Such relations, that is, socialize us in the sense that we needs must learn certain rightful relations beyond our own self-interest, and if the marriage is to go on, must acknowledge and act to some extent in accord with these relations. Men are thus pushed together by their needs; driven together by their insecurities even on the level of physical life.

This is not the full story, as we shall see, but it is an aspect which we must not minimize if we are to understand life. In most moral stages of development, goodness is never the incentive that evil is, nor has it an equal interest as news, because men are more driven by what they fear than drawn by what they love. Historic man, as a whole, is more conscious of the insecurities in his freedom than he is of the securities in his fellowship. That is why a new social situation is more of a problem than a pleasure to most people. Yet both the problem and the pleasure, of course, are generally present. Men are made for fellowship. They are not satisfied if left out. They want to be "in." They want to belong. They want to be socially useful and approved. On this psychological level of history, whether in small groups or as nations, introductions are not easy and natural. Nor is it easy to live together as good neighbors whether individually or nationally.

We want fellowship and freedom, security and independence, being approved and yet free to do as we please. We seek out and draw back. We hurt and we help. We include and we shut out. We are driven together by curiosity about our neighbors and we want to know what they think of us. Yet we want to be ourselves, too, and free to go our own way. In the conflict between these two drives we get into much trouble because we cannot act sensibly. We are too much driven by needs and insecurities which take on defensive thinking, rationalization, self-justification, blame of the other, criticism of the neighbor; we want to get along and to think of ourselves as all right. Yet often socially and internationally our fears conquer us and we are driven to say and to do things which hurt and which start conflicts.

We want and we do not want others. The conflicts within us seem to tempt us to ease them by externalizing them. Yet when once they are without we long for them to cease there, imagining that then we shall find peace. Evil leaders, themselves insecure, who play on the insecurities of men are listened to as realistic because they strike the deep note of man's actual situation, his fears that drive him, his needs that have turned into self-defensive and then into other-aggressive anxiety.

Men in history are also driven by fears of the ultimate. There is dread of the unknown. A child walking alone in the dark woods has experienced the eerie feeling of the dread unknown. It is not what can be seen. It is not the tops of the trees ahead as they outline the path against the sky. It is not the feel of the ground that barefoot feet grip. It is not the noises that are heard. It is that lurking danger. Each step feels its way with a vague sense that right ahead is a hole. Yet even the thought of a hole is too distinct. There is a vague sense of insecurity that accompanies each step and a distinct sense of relief when it is firmly planted. There is an eerie sense that something unexpected, not foreseen, may lurch forward from out of the half-hidden bushes next to the road. There is the lurking danger somewhere. What can be thought and seen, even the wolf in the imagination or the cry in the distance, is not to be compared to that uncanny something which lurks somewhere. The whole body is tense, ready, expectant. Any unexpected occurrence freezes and paralyzes the child until he gets some idea of what it is.

Man in history is a child in the dark. His religions are largely the rationalizations of his fears. He tries to read the riddle of the universe. In his depth-consciousness he questions even the outline of the trees against the sky. He wonders if he may not be off on a dangerous by-path. Others go by in the dimness and take other directions. Each step into the unknown is both a thrill and a dread. Fear is less the concrete content of things that threaten from without than a depth-anxiety within that historic man carries with him into the future.

Driven as he is by a will to live, to satisfaction, man is also fearful because he sees that all who walk at last fall over the edge. He is not certain where he is going, only that all roads end. Within his very deepest will to live, below conscious choice, is the basic, unavoidable frustration of it. The fear of death hangs ever over each man. His general sense of insecurity is symbolized by that final loss. History may move on. It may go somewhere. Yet he cannot go along. The ship of civilization may have a harbor; yet he and all whom he knows must be thrown overboard. Man wants to be free, to be secure, to be creative, to have satisfaction. All are threatened by the ultimate frustration of life itself.

Men search for security: in things, in positions, in friends, in doing right, in religions, even in costing religions. Men seek to forget: in pleasure, in work, in daydreaming, in artificial contests, and in destructive conflicts. Yet deep down is the fear of death. Men are born on a river above a cataract where the first edges of the waterfall reach far in to their birthplace. Some afterwards fall over the edge at two; others at ten; others at twenty; some float out on a long finger until they are eighty or ninety. Many drop alone. Many drop together in mass catastrophes, in some sudden eddy which swirls over and slings several boats over the edge. Men play and dance; they pray and sing; they work and visit. Yet deep in their lives is the sense of the end of it all—perhaps soon. The search for satisfaction is balanced this way and that by the sense of security. They cannot even be sure that the final fall is final. They have heard rumors that beyond is also a life. Of what nature? Is it better to perish or to live again? Man wonders, hopes, fears.

This dread of the unknown, the uncertain, coupled with the dread of death, the basic frustration of the will to live, increases man's basic sense of guilt. Man is a sinner. He feels deeply, though perhaps vaguely, that in relation to the ultimate he is not right. He wants to be, and yet he wonders if being right with the ultimate does not mean the surrender of the freedom which he treasures so much. He wonders if the surrender in religion will not itself be a basic frustration of the will to live, an escape, a surrender to his fears. If he is certain of the nature of the ultimate, more or less, he may dread even more what it requires. He cannot save life by sacrificing life, he feels. The fun in life, at least, seems gone. The ultimate may seem to require the surrender of his own plans, his kind of friendship, the structures of self-security which he has raised so painfully, both his having and his hoping. He may try to sacrifice something of what he has and wants, hoping that will do. Yet half right is not all right. He may try to deny that there is an ultimate. Yet deep down in man is this guilt feeling. Deep down he is driven by a sense of guilt. His thinking is considerably a fever philosophy.

Man's gods are greatly the creatures of his fears, whether in the image of his fears or in such shapes as are calculated to allay them. He hurts himself and takes pleasure in it by creating gods like unto himself who will understand and recognize the legitimacy of his motives. Or he sentimentalizes his gods into kind loves that will forgive and forget, letting him alone in his disobedience.

Man's history, even of religion, is the history of his fears, more than we know. That is why appeals to the ideal are largely futile. That is why appeals to reason are discouragingly useless. That is why facts will not convince. That is why the whole strategy of affecting history must be seen in the light of these fears of the ultimate, plus all the fears of the self, of society, of the world of nature, of mind, of body, and of the imagination of depth-response. Secondary fears become semi-independent or semi-autonomous traits of character or drives of life. Thus we feel guilty about the use of our time, our bodies, our minds; we feel guilty and anxious about our relations to society. We worry about the right of conventions over us and what people think of us. History is the history more than we think, of man's basic anxiety, ever becoming filled with concrete contents of fears and with the continual modification of these through the shifting days.

Yet man in history is not only *driven* toward fellowship—all the while he is also contrariwise driven by his will to independence, to freedom, to assert himself against the very fellowship that he craves—but he is also *drawn* to fellowship and a good deal pulled out of himself. Nor are these movements simply contradictory. Man stands between two tendencies, but not as though they were two distinct streams. They are rather all mixed up in conflicting eddies swirling forward and backward and toward all sides. Man is simply not a spirit in outright contradiction. Else he were not in a history cradled in nature and maturing through the environment of the flesh. Else were his acceptance or rebellion against God direct, outright. Contradiction is mixed, softened, but not made more bearable by being mixed with confusion. History is man in a confused contradiction between himself and God, himself and society, himself and his very interpretations of himself, God, society, and the nature which seems to mix into everything that he thinks or does. Thus toward nature, other men, and God, man is drawn by his very nature and by his situation in history, but drawn by a strong, slow, steady pull, obstructed by the drives, often much more concrete and violent, which tend the other way, yet which whirl about back and forth within the general confusion of man's contradictions, or pull as subtly as gravitation. The total aim of this contradiction is to make man feel both free and bound to

God and to his fellows, both free to develop individuality, thereby enriching the fellowship, and insecure enough not to allow him to feel independent, proud, or self-sufficient.

Men are actually mostly driven by their fears. Yet the deepest, the most essential, movement in the universe is the Love that draws. That underlies man's desire for satisfaction. That is the basis of his will to live. Self-satisfaction and self-will are self-frustrating. Without fellowship the individual fails to find freedom. Self-security deceives. There is none such. Men become disillusioned. To close in upon oneself is to close out true satisfaction. The fears that drive are the illusions of a false self. Here the Buddha is right. His deepest insights are peculiarly piercing. That is why his religion still lives. The estrangement of men from God and others is, however, only a temporary discipline that must be suffered for the sake of the rearing of real selves. Yet what drives us is but a back-surge that cannot withstand the tide of the drawing power of God's love. Individuation is for the sake of fellowship—primarily with God, and through Him with our fellow men.

Even in this life men are drawn by their physical, social, and spiritual environment. Men, in the first place, are drawn by the beauty of the physical world. After finishing the last section, the writer stood one evening watching a gorgeous October sunset. The air was crisp and clear, bathing the body in a refreshing tonic. The sky was both tense and still with color. It both burst and held. Val, the family German shepherd, scurried back and forth in great happiness. The writer could not help pondering theology and nature. This is how his thoughts ran:

Pity those who see no God in nature. Pity those who, because hail, for instance, might destroy, can see mostly evil in the world upon which God looked and called it good. Nature may be cursed for man's sake, but, like life, the good in it far outweighs the bad. It is both untrue and ungrateful to say aught else. One does not compliment the God of revelation by separating Him from His creation. Beauty is an intrinsic but generally far understressed aspect of God's revelation of Himself. His handiwork is wondrous to behold. The flowers, the woods, the mountains and the seas, the soil that bears the harvest, the trees that yield fruit, the rocks made into fences, the lumber that shelters, the oil that lets us visit, the steam and the electric power that work for us—how good are not the works of the Lord!

To lie on the ground and work in the soil and not feel the deeper rhythm, to row on the water and not sense the deeper presence, to fly in the air and not commune with a higher sphere is to be unaware of the farthest reaches of physical existence. Nature may have been sentimentalized by some poets and its hardships may not have been sufficiently appreciated. Yet dull are those who shovel the newly fallen snow with a grudge in their heart. Some do it with an inner thrill and with a sense of mystery, of holy communion. This sense is due to no condition of body or circumstance, either. Dull are those who see bushes and no flames. Dull are we when the trees and the blades of grass have not darting out from them the silver rays of God's invariable presence in them. In the Spirit all nature is truly seen. Without the Spirit we go through God's universe blindfolded. There is a communing with animals as God's creatures which is deeper than language.

We live like blind people. Occasionally our eyes are opened and then we marvel at the very beauty of the world which we have never seen before although we have looked at it a million times. In the Spirit even dead bodies are not repulsive; they were the faithful, hard-tasked servants of spirits now freed for fuller service. They were called to a particular task. Now they return to their home in God's more general realm. He who walks through nature driven by fear meets enemies and dangers everywhere. He who walks through nature with God breathes mostly the fresh air, picks flowers, and works with creative freshness in the zest of exuberant youth. The Spirit is eternally young, rested, and fresh. The more we live in God the less anxiety and the more abundant life we feel. Except as we are blinded by our un-Christian fears of danger and death, our physical environment draws. Its friendliness and usefulness speak, saying: "Here you cannot stay. You have a better home. Yet see the beauty and the goodness of the world, though abused by man, and surrender in faithful peace your total security to Him who made this and who waits only till you are ready, according to His plan for each and all, to make a fitter nature for you."

Even need and physical catastrophe tend to bring people together. Many barriers were broken down in the London subways during the blitz. Pioneer farmers who had to help each other and had to borrow from each other developed many a strong tie of friendship. In the zero hour on the battle front when physical danger had to be faced, many found themselves turning to God and seeing each other with barriers down. When common danger threatens a community, through pestilence or hurricane, through flood or war, men are driven back on their common humanity, and, not infrequently, on their common dependence as a humanity on forces beyond themselves. At the funeral service there can be sensed a common depth-situation. The precariousness, needs and dangers of life thus show not only the evils of our situation but also a common, and often victorious, facing of those evils.

Our abuse of nature is far worse than nature's abuse of us, for its purpose is not to provide permanent security or satisfaction. Its basic purpose is precisely *precariousness*. We are pilgrims on the earth. What is worse still is "man's inhumanity to man" and his divisive loyalties. The precariousness of nature is for our good according to the Purpose of process, the highest truth that we know. Through the demonic forces and situations of life, moreover, work not only the fears of men but also their faiths. Often humanity, confronted by the dangers and death due to the conditions of nature, rises to heights of heroism that can only be marveled at. The pilot sticks with his plane and is burned rather than risk by his bailing out the possible killing of someone else on the ground.

That brings us to the fact that people have considerable native good in them. There is a grace of creation as well as of redemption! Men are drawn together by men, on the social level as well as by nature. There is good in men by creation which draws to itself. Abstract theologies calling themselves realistic tend to deny this. But fact it is, fact unshakable. Humanity, to be sure, is more driven by its fears than drawn by its loves, but fear and ill will are not what men want. Men are hemmed in by fears. They are caught, dominated by them. They feel insecure and defensive. Even Christian leaders take for granted defensive feelings and sufferings in the exceptional few who hardly ever feel them. They are so common as to be almost unconsciously attributed even to "the saints." The very sympathy of these Christian leaders reveals how they themselves would feel under the same circumstances.

Yet let people experience genuine love. Let them become convinced that one is seeking their good authentically and without debate. They often respond like grateful puppies. They open up like wilting flowers in a shower. Few saints there have been in history. How even they have known their shortcomings. Yet how mankind has responded; it craves to worship such people, although they themselves crave to point beyond themselves. They speak with an authority beyond words and formulas.

Even without these special keys, these Christian witnesses, to unlock the hearts of men in their inner chambers, there is an astounding amount of sheer thoughtfulness and friendliness in the world. Often it is shy; often it is clumsy; often it wonders if it is presumptuous and will be "taken" right; often it is stifled by our defensive fears. Yet the fact is certain that men are made for fellowship; their freedom becomes empty without it; without social approval, admiration, attention, personal independence becomes a most lonely and undesirable thing. Some seek it selfishly and find no peace or security. Others seek wholeness *within* the fellowship of God's family, and find lasting satisfaction.

God has not left Himself without a witness in any human soul, however twisted and warped. The grain of the Maker's wood is the basic structure, however overlaid by other material may be the pieces. A dog on a walk will run to meet another dog, the tail half-waving and the hackles half-rising—half-friendly, half aggressive. Yet they *will* meet, and soon they fight or play. More often they play, too, than fight. So also is mankind. We want each other. We need each other. We usually like each other when we really know each other and when we understand more fully why we all talk and act the way we do. We are naturally friendly unless threatened by insecurity, physical, social, or spiritual. Evil, even in our short history, can be seen as that which thwarts the effecting of the fellowship for which God is making us. Actuality may, however, be broken by essentiality. Our proper selves may yield to the potential. Most evil comes from our refusal to accept this ideal fellowship which is our true essentiality. We refuse mostly because we are afraid. Yet we do it also because we have enjoyed finite power and falsely and sinfully have perverted it into infinite pride, into an attempted self-sufficiency over against God and others. Yet deeper than both fear and pride lies the truth of what we essentially are and shall become, namely, the children of God, members of His family, fellows in His fellowship.

Sin is simply not merely a direct denial of God's will. That must be stressed. We are men, not devils. No devil, even, has infinite power like God to deny Him directly. All rebellion against God is finite. We are dragged down by all the weaknesses of the flesh. Even when we surrender ourselves fully to God as best we know, there seems to be the sin which still persists in us. There is a body of death which simply is not ourselves. Call it *libido* as opposed to the *ego*. Call it flesh as opposed to the spirit. Call it anything. The fact is there. We are weak, finite creatures. We are fearful. We are insecure. We want to trust God. Yet faith may be "the task of a life-time." We surrender, we feel, wholly only to be importunate widows, knocking, knocking. Deep anxieties and pulls steal up under our very hearts. Must the body die, as the

Buddhists believe, before the spirit can be set fully free? We have victories, long stretches of victory, only to feel again the grip of fear or the pain of suspicion. Why is this? It may become weaker and weaker. But why at all? Is it God's patient discipline of our souls?

Our rebellion is certainly not pure pride. It is often a confused attempt to be sufficient in ourselves because we are not clear about what there is to hang together with safely. There are many gods and the One we need may not always have a clear countenance. He often comes to us in the dark and wrestles with us and we cry: "What is thy name?" There is pride, to be sure. There is arrogance, of course. There is definitely a defying of God. There is sin as the knowing good and doing it not. There is refusal of the Christian fellowship by those who know what it is. Yet the situation is mixed. There is often legitimate seeking for satisfaction, misconceived and misdirected. Pride must not be made the chief or only explanation of sin. Pride is primarily due to a faithlessness which is both guilty and not guilty, to a basic anxiety within our experience which exists for a purpose.

Our putting ourselves at the center is pedagogically necessary and as such is demonic rather than satanic. When the temptation, which is necessary, but not yielded to by natural necessity, in an invariable or non-optional sense, becomes the occasion for letting ourselves be mastered by sin, that sin is a complex of rightful desire to be ourselves, to satisfy our needs, insecurity, and resulting faithlessness, the drag down of nature in us, "our animal heritage," *and* the willful acceptance of the evil which tempts us, mixed with confusion; we thus being partly overcome by evil as well as accepting it. We start falsely with a perfect Adam, the First and the Second, instead of with our animal and human continuity. Yet decisive discontinuity, transforming our continuity, is from above our explanatory rather than our existential continuity.

Yet the opposite to the full grace of God is not full willful rebellion but rather this mixed situation. The full continuity of

perspective and process is from God down, never from us up.
When men are so understood we can sympathize with them deeply
as well as hold them both pedagogically and existentially responsible. God forgives both because men are penitent and because
they know not what they do. He remembers not only His faithfulness to forgive but also that we are dust. Only growth in both
grace and truth can produce full penitence, forgiveness, and the
fellowship yielding the fruits of the Spirit.

Modern theology is in danger of taking man the creature and
his sin too seriously, not existentially, but in his understanding of
it. Modern theology is threatened with a false pragmatism, of reducing God's being and purpose unintentionally to what may seem
to cause crises of repentance. Men will not hear, however, if what
they hear does not correspond with what they feel to be true in
the depths of their own lives. Compassion is still the deepest cure
both for weakness and for sin. Men do not want to be selfish, sinners; they cannot recognize themselves as sheer rebels; they want
to live, to have their needs met. They want fellowship, but fellowship in which they can be creatively free and constructively secure. They are not altogether sure that some preaching does make
the more abundant life available to them. True theology must
explain as well as exhort; it must offer truth as well as grace.

The spiritual environment, too, draws, as well as the physical
and the social. Religions are largely the product of fear, at least
quantitatively speaking, because men are more driven by fears than
drawn by love, explicitly and directly, at this stage of their development. Yet the highest in all religions is salvation, or release
of some kind, from those fears. Who can read the Tao Tê Ching
or the Bhagavad-Gita and not be struck by their drawing power?
Here is spiritual insight and advice on a high level which attracts.
Here is the lure of the ideal. Who can ponder the power of Gau-
tama Buddha and not see how the key to his hold over the
masses is his teaching of practical redemption from the fears and
illusions of self? His own compassion for men in renouncing per-

sonal release for the sake of telling others the way of escape, legendary though the shell of the story may be, is one of the high spots of human history. There is no reason to think that it does not represent a genuine attribute of his character who has drawn over the ages the multitudes of sufferers unto himself. Those scriptures which are dearest to people in all living religions are the passages which draw men; these are lifted up and out from the rest of the scriptures and made into living keys to judge and interpret the rest.

When Christ is lifted up he draws all men unto himself—Christ the compassionate, Christ the sufferer for our sake, Christ the healer of our hearts. That God loved until He gave has become the summary, the little Bible, of the Christian faith. Our Roman Catholic friends have in large numbers taken to the worship of Mary because she understands and sympathizes with them concretely. Even if the Father and the Son could give up for eternity the lost sons of men, the tender love of Mary, the Mother of God, refuses to surrender her own. Hume and others may tell us that fear explains historically the rise of religions. This may be quantitatively true, the largest actual source. Yet the high points of the religions, their drawing cards, are the points of hope, compassion, and friendliness. Pick up Alcoran, for example, and read heading after heading: "In the name of the most merciful God."[3]

History is best understood through the study of men's religions because their religions represent their whole-interpretations of their universe. To know what people actually worship, to understand what they deem existentially most important and most real, is most fully to understand them where they live most deeply. The history of religions is the pilgrimage of man from the land of fear where armies of defense try in vain to make the self feel free and secure through the lowlands of disillusionment and despair to the land of faith, the high unguarded country, in-

[3] On this point Champion has done a peculiarly significant work in *The Eleven Religions*.

accessible to human assaults, and therefore also quite unprotected from them. From the lowlands one can reach the land of faith only by being drawn up from above. Those who have passed from self-security through self-despair to God-security have already tasted the meaning of history and reckon the trouble on the road as nothing in comparison to the delight of the land. Man can and must be driven into the lowlands of despair, driven by his own foolishness and fears, but any time he can let himself be drawn, once there, up to the land of faith, up into the freedom and security of a God-grounded fellowship.

History is thus of a kind to provide a key to the solution of the kinds of evil that we know. Through fear and faith history has been built providing the conditions necessary, under God, for the transmutation of experience into good on the personal-spiritual level. Several problems about history itself nevertheless remain pertaining precisely to the conditions of this personal-spiritual level.

CHAPTER XI

Death and the End of History

History here, for instance, is beset by unavoidable frustrations. At best it can constitute a beginning only. By hope we must be saved. History at best provides only proximate ends for any and all individuals. There is for all the fact of death. If evil is defined as frustration of the fellowship, here is the deepest and most final frustration. As far as actuality goes, here is the end for everyone of history itself.

In whatever direction men march they all must reach one lowland, the lowland of death. That is history's, as well as nature's, final frustration. Our souls, that is, the total capacities and contents of our human consciousness, die. That valley of despair, death, no one can escape. In this life men are fooled by the false securities which they work so hard to build. This life ends and with it all securities in the self and in this world. Death is the unavoidable valley of despair for all men, unless before it they have found their God-security. The problem of life has its fuller and final setting in the problem of death, our eighth area.

Death is the shock of the self-sufficient self, the fulfillment of his worst fears. Death is the total frustration of the will to live and to self-satisfaction apart from the will of God. Death is the denuding of each one who hides from God. Even the fig leaves of man's modesty are stripped away to reveal that not modesty but sin was the reason for the clothing. The evil was not without, not of the body; it was within, in the heart. Clothing is good for shelter from the cold and to individuate us in our fellowships; yet clothing may also be a symbol of the evil heart and the evil eye. Clothing hides not from God. Death is the total darkening of our selfish hopes and of our greedy graspings.

Death is the worst enemy to the natural man and the best friend to the self to be. Death is the terror of total individuality. Death is all-aloneness. Death is a river that drowns each individual completely. Yet death is also the door to hope. Death is the invitation to a new kind of life. Death is a new start. Death is the beginning of a *new history*. Death is the divine shock treatment to restore spiritual sanity. Death is the burning of God's holiness separating each one from all he held dear—that he might meet God and his true destiny. Death is a corridor, a dark tunnel, where we see ourselves at once in all our history and in our total situation.

The drowning man has had an anticipation of death. In death our lives are weighed with true scales by a perfect weigher. Death is the testifier to the fact that men cannot go on smoothly resisting God. God shifts the pace. God puts on the fuller pressure. According to each man's life is the meaning of his death. Death is the bright hope of God's fuller history for each man according to His wonderful wisdom, and perhaps for each generation, or for each history as a whole. Though the soul dies, the Spirit lives. The natural man, the capacities and the contents, that is, of his consciousness, perishes. No one is naturally immortal. The Spirit is given new life by the grace of God, and such capacities and contents, old and new, as He in His wisdom and love selects.

Christian faith finds death, therefore, to be a big factor in the solution of the problems of evil. Naturally there is no solution at all that amounts to anything except as a rationalization, however ingenious, unless there is a prolongation after death of our essential lives. Truth tells us that there is. The reflexive superspective is the Christian God. He is not a "God of the dead, but of the living."[1] "Love can never lose its own."[2]

The God who made this wonderful world of which we see now but the merest beginning, the God who showed himself most fully in the decisive event of history, the life of Jesus, the God of perfect power and love, will perfect with all certainty that which He has here barely begun. These statements are obviously and definitely from the perspective of the reflexive superspective. They are the upshot of faith and reason in their dynamic synthesis. They cannot be fully proved, by the nature of the case, but they follow forcefully from the central meaning we see. They are intrinsic and inevitable to Christian faith. They are the pointings of process whereby we can both understand it most fully and live in it most victoriously.

We do not want to say much about death and immortality, particularly in this volume, except that they are subject to the same severity and goodness of God as we know here. Yet so great a discontinuity is death and so different is the fullness of God's purpose and way of working from our best understanding that the best that we can do, at least until fuller light breaks, is to leave the particulars of the subject beyond the limits of faith.[3] We know God and His love for us. We know that we shall live in a fuller existence for our own good, whether under conditions of far greater severity than here, or in the new heavens which we await according to His promise. To know that much is enough. The fact of death, the great redemptive discontinuity, and of the new life are powerful spurs to a faster race to do the wonderful will of God in order to attain for all as well as for ourselves the things which are far better than we can now ask or think.

[1] Matthew 22:32.

[2] Whittier, *Snow-Bound.*

[3] Joseph Fort Newton in *River of Years* makes the beautiful observation that while faith is for the young, trust is for the old.

As far as "the click" of insight goes, the self-authenticating illumination of the spirit, the problem of evil cannot be fully solved even in trust until we have learned to think of death as a friend, until life's precariousness is entirely from the loving hand of God, at least as a kind of condition; even though the contents of that condition may not be directly from God. Our son may die more directly because of man's sinfulness or more indirectly because of the working of God's general providence, but this kind of world is for our own good and such death severs not from God. Death is an incident in the generous economy of God which makes it possible for Him in this life to grant a freedom which is itself also fully conditioned and controlled for our fullest eventual good. To think mostly in terms of our lives before our kind of death is to think in such squeezed terms as most certainly to preclude any adequate solution of the problem of evil.

The deepest solutions, anyway, are not in thought but in the spirit. Those who suffer, incurably ill, often embody the fullest answer. What matters most in life is not how we explain but how we accept suffering. Having accepted it, we find a new light breaking through. The God seen through eyes that have long been washed by tears is far fairer than the one seen from the bed of ease. To accept suffering as a gift from God *to be used for others* is hard, but suffering so accepted opens the door to a new world and to the real God. To those who have not had and do not want such experiences, this saying is an offense. Those who know long, dedicated suffering, have a kind of knowledge that stands severe tests of thought and tends to ·pierce more and more through the fogs of our human lowlands. To such knowledge, death is neither a chasm nor a wall, but a door. Beyond, the fuller and truer history *starts*.

Yet have we not got away from history as a means of understanding the why of evil? Are we not rather dealing with individuals? Is not history a collective entity? History cannot be dealt with adequately except in terms of both its meaning as a whole and its meaning for individuals. History as a whole has not a self-sufficient meaning. History is the story of men before God and with each other. As men before God they are individuals in a certain sense apart from their direct connection with others. Kierkegaard has a point in saying that men are individuals only as they are freed from the universal in the direct religious situation. Yet no one lives unto himself alone. To be truly before God is to be a man with barriers down between him and his fellow men. We can never know either God or men unless we forgive, unless we give ourselves to others. Barriers between ourselves and others, on our part, if we refuse to let God break them down, are also barriers between God and us. We thereby shut ourselves into a self-circle away from all deep and direct fellowship. To understand the meaning of history is to know how men both become truly themselves and also become themselves only in the security of a God-centered fellowship. It is to see in what way individuals become saved finally as well as to see the purpose of the historical development as a whole.

We cannot, therefore, ignore either individual destiny or the destiny of history as a whole. Defensive thinking, dreading personal responsibility and accountability, often likes to think that when we die we are lost in some spiritual ocean. This may represent a profound insight, defensively distorted. Our little crowns of consciousness are shallow and intermittent. We sleep, take ether, are "knocked out." Where are we then? How does consciousness in individual selves depend upon bodily behavior and how upon the spirit as a whole beyond the individual? There are undoubtedly depths of the self which are even now at one with mankind. There are undoubtedly more depths of the self still which are even now latent in God. History is like a body with other cells and with God's life as an entirety. We may soon discover depths in man as different in capacity as the solar energy of the atomic bomb is from our regular electrical energy.

We may go far beyond that. We may be on the brink of a new

age of man, a new evolution, a new kind of consciousness, in terms of which we may differ more from our present selves than we do now from the animal world. Telepathy and prayer, for instance, may be far better understood as we come to understand man better. Perhaps just as a hypodermic in the arm, or an injection of antibodies, helps the whole body, or a specific sick part not in the arm, our prayers can constitute the cellular space where God's hypodermic needle pierces the skin of history, yet helps in some other place where it is needed.

There is a fellowship of suffering, a fellowship of co-operation, a fellowship of guilt, a fellowship of grace, and a fellowship of the spirit far deeper than our little conscious selves. In such a way life after death may find us far more closely linked, far differently linked, far more organically intertwined. The separateness of our present kind of individuality may not characterize the future life. There may be a degree of freedom and of creative individuality which is also different in kind from our present state. Just as we are more individuals than animals by means of our kind of consciousness, we may find ourselves in a new and higher individuality, yet even so far more deeply one in a new relation of the spirit which is now entirely hid from our eyes. Yet this legitimate thought should not be used as an excuse for self-indulgence and for a lack of personal responsibility. Whatever the relation as to a new kind of individuality and community, we are linked in God through a responsible concern for each and all.

Yet the problem of history as a whole, even beyond this, clamors for some kind of solution. Why should there be progress in history while all individuals drop out of it and cannot profit any more from it? History goes on. The generations perish. We sometimes feel like Kierkegaard:

> One generation can learn much from another, but that which is purely human no generation can learn from the preceding generation. In this respect every generation begins again from the beginning, possessing no other tasks but those of the preceding gen-

erations and going no further, unless the preceding generation has betrayed itself and deceived itself. . . . No generation has learned how to love from another, no generation begins at any other point than the beginning, and no subsequent generation has a shorter task than the generation which preceded it.[4]

If each and every generation must begin all over again, why should there be any progress at all in history as a whole? On the other hand, if it is possible for some to begin higher up in the scale of evolution than others, why did not creation begin there in the first place?

That there is progress in history as a whole is indisputable if we want to look open-mindedly at the facts—progress, that is, from the point of view of the most high and the most real. We must not look too closely at ten years, or at ten hundred years. We must get a little more adequate perspective: inorganic life, life, consciousness, self-consciousness, human history, religion, the highest pinnacle of faith and vision. That is a truer perspective.

The coming of the Hebrew prophets, Jesus, and the New Testament added something better than before to history, at least improving its possibilities for improvement. Never before, too, has the highest as an ideal been as widely known and challenging as

[4] *Fear and Trembling*, pp. 183-184. He makes the point that no one can go beyond love and faith. True. Yet has there not been immense progress in the understanding of both? Is love the same, for instance, after Jesus as before? Has there been no understanding of faith and love developed since then, for instance, in hospitals and in social service? Has not the Christian fellowship within a hundred years had its first widespread inkling of how concretely and consistently the Gospel must be applied to all spheres of life? Kierkegaard has himself expressed this truth well, for instance, in *The Concept of Dread*: "It hardly need be said that this view is not chargeable with any sort of Pelagianism, which lets every individual, unconcerned about the race, play his own little history in his private theater; for the history of the race calmly pursues its course, and in this no individual commences at the same place as another, whereas every individual begins afresh and at that same instant is at the place where he ought to begin in history." (pp. 31-32). Cf. also for an interesting discussion Gerald Heard's *The Eternal Gospel*, pp. 20 ff.

now. Universal education and comunication are setting the stage for a new possible spread of a religion that will give us freedom with security, fellowship with creative individuality. The world is getting to be a unit of circumstance in which we are both driven and drawn by terrible fears and the high invitation of the Christ to be one through the freeing power of faith in God. The stakes are higher than ever before, and in both opposition and victory Christ calls.

This does not mean that progress in this world is necessary. We may fail our chance as a history and be destroyed. It does not mean that progress is automatic apart from the point of view of our personal and social acceptance of the ways of God. But the fact is and remains that there has been this development as a whole in history and that the stage is even now set for a new abundance in every realm of life—if only we will accept what is offered. In the long perspective there has been progress in the highest truth we know: the preparing for, effecting, and widening the Christian fellowship. Latourette's painstaking volumes of investigation can hardly be ignored or gainsaid at this point. Yet why this progress if no individual and no generation can partake of it? If some of us can start here, moreover, why not start the whole process here in the first place?

There is no solution to this problem, that we can see, if we accept the idea that every individual and every generation starts at scratch. The problem, however, is not so simple as that. They do, and they do not. They do in that no individual and no generation can avoid going through for itself the whole process of history from our individuation by our attempt at self-security to the fellowship which comes when self-despair is allowed to be changed by the love and the power of God into God-security. This process is necessary for one and for all, the whole of it. No one can inherit outright either love or faith. For all progress in the understanding of love and faith, moreover, there is also some corresponding evil. Life and history are demonic, that is, all their good is generally mixed or threatened with evil. The higher the development is, too, the deeper is its evil.

The inheritance of *the conditions* for love and for faith, furthermore, is not the same thing as the inheritance of faith and love. In this respect Kierkegaard is right, and this point must be stressed over and over again. Every person must become the religious individual. That is too often glossed over most superficially in our nominal Christianity. In personal faith, hope, and love individuals in the past may have gone far deeper than any and all "moderns." There is no way of telling. There is no way of measuring this, of thus comparing progress. God only knows that.

A philosopher of religion who is reported to have said that he was necessarily better than Jesus because, living after him, he had the advantage (poor Jesus) of Jesus' knowledge, of all subsequent interpretation of Jesus' knowledge, of all creative imitation, of all subsequent creativity plus all new knowledge, particularly the scientific method which Jesus never knew—seems in this respect to have missed the meat of the matter. There simply is no short cut to the kingdom of Heaven. The whole process is necessary. In a most important personal sense every individual must begin the whole process afresh. Each one must recapitulate the heights of the past, if he is ever to go beyond it. That is why history is no automatic machine. That is why it is no escalator of progress. That is why evil persists of every kind and why new goods are perverted by personal decision into worse evils than ever.

Yet even though there is no individual progress in the sense that anyone can escape going the whole way from individual rebellion to the fellowship of suffering and the fellowship of salvation, there is nevertheless progress in the conditions or the possibilities for fellowship whereby each individual and each generation can go beyond the preceding one. Whole-response includes knowledge and knowledge is a social act. The structure and the content of experience both individual and social are enlarged in this respect. Recapitulation has a profound truth to teach us, whether it be theologically as in Irenaeus or psychologically as in G. Stanley Hall, namely, that all advanced life is cumulative. There is an inheritance of knowledge, of understanding, of the interpretation of experience, of the larger environment, which makes it possible for an individual to recapitulate and vicariously to appropriate in his own experience the experience of the past. The past was necessary. There is no automatic growth. Abraham, for instance, inherited at least thought forms, speech, and the beginnings of religious understanding and devotion. There is such a thing as social inheritance in this sense. We can profit from past growth. Jesus drew much knowledge and inspiration from the prophets. He knew and loved much of the Old Testament. His life was discontinuity built on continuity.

Thus there can be progress in history as a whole because in this recapitulation and advance the conditions and helps for fellowship can be improved and enlarged. The later fellowship may not be deeper in intensity, but it is deeper and more meaningful in content, provided that it be, of course, personally appropriated. Intensity often even lessens while the thought content widens. Intensity is often due to defensive narrowness. There must, therefore, be a preparation for the Gospel if the Gospel is to arrive both meaningfully and without voiding the compossible ways of God, which cannot be. This is true, we repeat, even for the Son, who has behind him the prophetic preparation. Mary is one symbol of all that lay behind Jesus. John the Baptist is another. The remarkable passages about Mary must not be left out of account if we are fully to understand the life of Jesus. The births of John and of Jesus similarly ought to be read together. The ones who were later to understand the Gospel and to pass it on also needed the fellowship of the early church which produced the New Testament.

We need the past as objectified in the Bible. Abraham may have had as much faith as Jesus, but between him and Jesus were, for instance, men like Hosea, Jeremiah, the Second Isaiah, and the writer of the Book of Jonah. The higher the conditions, more-over, the fuller the sin and the harder the struggle. Evil grows with the good except as, and until, the latter overcomes the for-mer in personally and socially decisive fashion. That requires the power of God to make effectual the fellowship in the Gospel of the grace of God.

This fellowship on the higher levels, moreover, can never be had apart from the struggles of *every* level. In the case of the newer generations the process is simply speeded up. History is both demonic and divine, but the stronger of these is the second. The sin against the fuller and brighter light hardens and hurts the self and others more than the sin against the dimmer and the narrower light. Yet the higher good, on the other hand, also has greater power to eradicate evil. For this reason it is a good thing, and not a neutral or a bad condition, that the homes, the schools, and the churches of each generation be as good as possible. Only in this way can there be real advance in fellowship. God it is who works in this way. Although, consequently, every higher good has its deeper evil, let us also remember that this means that every higher evil has its own higher good still. Evil is but a per-version. It is adjectival. It is a by-product of the fellowship process, not automatically of progress, at least as such, but the partly free choice of our personal situation.

Who knows, furthermore, if in the next life we may not find this history reversed? Who knows if the phrase "that they with-out us should not be made perfect," "they" meaning the preced-ing generations, not only means that the fellowship as a whole, that is, history as a whole, is not perfected except as we go on from where they were—we first needing, of course, to get where they were—but means also, actually, that in the next life we must somehow serve those generations from which we are now benefit-ing. We read in the Bible that Jesus preached to those who were in hell.[5] That is a most meaningful and suggestive insight, slipped

[5] "In prison"; I Peter 3:19-20.

perhaps symbolically from the depths of God's work in the sub-conscious. In hell he gave the opportunity of the new knowledge and the new power of salvation to those who did not previously know it.

Is this a true symbol for the workings of history as a whole of which he is the abiding center? Will history in one vital sense be judged as a whole? Are we all so much a community that no one can be saved, at least fully and finally saved, until we are all saved? This would be both a just and an organic way of treating history. This would tie in the generations from one end to the other, not only in one direction but in both. It seems likely that personal and communal responsibility and grace will be merged in some greater transgenerational responsibility and grace until God has completed His whole council with this our process. The end of our earthly history may be near. The new necessity of finding our security in God if we are not to destroy history on earth may cause such a turning to God as the world has never seen.

It may be that the gears of God for our history will be shifted still faster, into His super-high, and that the millennium will come on earth in God's dramatic way. Those are surely misjudging the power of God to control history who leave out this possibility. The victorious end of history may be nearer than we dare to dream, much less believe. God may even in our day be forcing a decision. We take for granted that we will, must, have a future. That fascinating last book of the Bible, Revelation, may not be merely the description of the experience of the early Church, as it is fashionable to believe in scholarly circles. It may truly describe prophetically and predictively the end of our earthly epoch. Our smooth continuity of liberal thought may suddenly be shattered on the hard rock of God's action in history. Will man shortly destroy himself, unlocking ever new secrets that he cannot, or will not, control, defying heaven? Will but a remnant of mankind remain after the Armageddon of some next war, a fraction of the world being burned, etc?

We have built too safely on the sands of human predictability. We have thought that proximate ends can be had without regard to the ultimate. We have laid the foundations of our thought on human and historic actualities far more than on the power of God in His sovereign majesty. We were to remake history in terms of mostly gradual progress. Any discontinuity in history had to be slight and by all means forward. God may plunge forward by plunging our whole history to destruction. We fail to grasp God's use of catastrophe. Perhaps part of history will perish as a sin-offering, not twenty or a million people but hundreds of millions, while the remaining part becomes radically changed. History may, of course, simply keep crawling along, snailing along, both while we live and for numberless generations ahead. But the end may even now be in sight. The day of the Lord may be today, darkness and not light, or the light of the new earth wherein dwelleth righteousness. Those seem foolish who predict too minutely the ways of God. We have no final basis on which to judge God's future and final way with our history. They are not our ways. That we know. They are not in our dimension of being and purpose. The gears are shifted from above. In the end God will have His way, and in His way.

CHAPTER XII

Evil and Last Things

Whether or no this history ends within our compass of thinking, we know that in God's time our kind of history will have
an end: God's predetermined end. "God hath shut up all unto disobedience, that he might have mercy upon all:"[1] "If we are faithless, he abideth faithful; for he cannot deny himself."[2] In the
end God's will shall be done on earth as in heaven, whether on this
our earth or on a new earth according to His promise. The God
who is our Lord and Love in Jesus Christ knows how to conquer
all principalities and powers, all heights and depths, all things
present and things to come. In the end He will subject all things
to Himself, His perfect Agape-love winning out, that He might
be all in all. He wants all to be saved, and His wants are never
vain. He wants to have all His children loving and understanding
sons that to endless time they might enjoy the family fellowship.

Without the ultimate salvation of all creatures, men and, we
think, animals, in God's time and way, it is easy to see that there
can be no full solution of the problem of evil. Even if the "evil"
perish there is loss and shortcoming in God's work. There is
waste of the creative life of God. If there were an eternal hell,
God's love would, of course, unquestionably be finite. Traditional-
istic theology has proclaimed either an evil or a finite God. We

[1] Romans 11:32.
[2] II Timothy 2:13.

117

must above all have a worthy view of God. Consider the wise words of St. Athanasius without the unnatural limitations of traditional theology:

> Surely it would have been better never to have been created at all than, having been created, to be neglected and perish; and, besides that, such indifference to the ruin of His own work before His very eyes would argue not goodness in God but limitation, and that far more than if He had never created men at all. It was impossible, therefore, that God should leave man to be carried off by corruption, because it would be unfitting and unworthy of Himself.[3]

The logic of the situation is simple. Either God could not or would not save all. If He could not He is not sovereign; then not all things are possible with God.[4] If He would not, again the New Testament is wrong, for it openly claims that He would have all to be saved.[5] Nor would He be totally good.

Let us not base the conclusion, however, solely on New Testament grounds. The witness of the New Testament is inconclusive except to the kind of literalist who fastens upon a certain verse, waves his Bible, and shouts, "It says so!" while conveniently forgetting such emphatic pasages as Romans, Chapters 3 through 11, which begins by asserting that the faithlessness of some cannot nullify the faithfulness of God,[6] and ends by saying that God has consigned all men to disobedience that He might have mercy upon all.[7] The total logic of the deepest message of the New Testament, namely, that God both can and wants to save all, is unanswerable.

On the grounds of our total analysis of truth, moreover, our existential ultimate requires that all be saved, or else Agape is

[3] St. Athanasius, *The Incarnation of the Word of God* (Centenary Press edition, 1944), p. 32.
[4] Matthew 19:26 and Mark 10:27.
[5] I Timothy 2:4.
[6] Romans 3:3.
[7] Romans 11:32.

not ultimate. Otherwise the most high is not fully the most real. Man's freedom is no excuse. God has both created it and conditioned it according to His loving wisdom and power. He also controls it for our good.

If one creature is to be eternally tormented, Christ's compassion declares that it were far better that there had been no creation. Yet God knew what He did when He created the world. "Creation is the inbreaking and revelation of divine compassion," writes Barth.[8] "Christian faith knows better than all optimisms that the last word about the created world is positive and not negative."[9] God's participation in the negative aspect of existence is only that of a moment.[10] The Christian faith has an unshakable assurance in the perfection of existence—because it is God's.[11] It is not only good in its totality but the best and for the best.[12] The Christian sees beyond the evils by a free and joyous seeing, by a sure seeing, in spite of present evils, in the light of God's revelation. "From this foundation he sees through the imperfection of existence to its perfection."[13] Only a view like this can be worthy of God's power and Christ's compassion.

If hell were eternal, furthermore, heaven would be an eternal place of mourning. All those truly in the Agape fellowship would identify their lot with the lost. The fuller the love, the deeper the suffering in sympathy with the irrevocably and irreparably lost. That is why we have said elsewhere that heaven can be heaven only when it has emptied hell.

With respect to this question, so-called Christian theology is

[8] Barth, *Die Kirchliche Dogmatik*, Dritter Band, Erster Halbband, p. 122. "*Schöpfung heisst Einbruch und Offenbarung des göttlichen Erbarmens.*"

[9] *Ibid.*, p. 443. "*Der christliche Glaube weiss aber besser als aller Optimismus, dass das letzte Wort über die Geshöpfwelt ein positives und nicht ein negatives ist.*"

[10] Cf. *ibid.*, p. 440.

[11] Cf. *ibid.*, pp. 445-446.

[12] Cf. *ibid.*, p. 443.

[13] *Ibid.*, p. 435. "*Von dieser Grundlage her sieht er durch die Unvollkommenheit des Daseins hindurch in seine Vollkommenheit.*"

still too much hemmed in by fear and invidious comparison. Even if we make our bed in hell God is there.[14] The love of God must ever preach to those in prison.[15] That Kansas man of God, George Allison, once preached on the idea that when we build the Church on the confession that Jesus Christ is the Son of God and live that confession, even the gates of hell shall not be able to withstand it. We are likely to think of evil as on the offensive and the Church as on the defensive. When, however, the Church becomes truly Christian, evil cannot entrench itself even behind the gates of hell. These barricades, too, will at last give way.

Yet hell does exist. Hell is the insurmountable barrier between heaven and the hardened heart. But the heart need not *stay* hardened. No one can get to heaven apart from complete self-despair. God will never, to be sure, force direct surrender. To paraphrase an old Gospel song, He will not compel us to go against our will; He will just make us willing to go. He will make our own way so self-punishing that at last we come to our better selves and see how good for us is His way. By our own choices and experiences we shall become willing and loving children of God. In this life, of course, we see the mere beginning of this process. How many surprises we are to meet in ages beyond this life!

True preaching, to those who do not live as sons of the Father, must always be, "Except ye repent, ye shall all likewise perish."[16] For the wayward heart this is the only truth. In the direction in which he is going, away from God, lie increasing difficulty, ever diminishing satisfaction, mounting suffering and sorrow. Yet mere fear will not cause genuine repentance. The severity of God must be backed in teaching and example by His goodness, which leads to repentance. He who is insecure dares not let go unless he sees better footing. The full Gospel, including both severity and goodness, is ever necessary if we are truly to help and to save.

---

[14] Psalm 139:8.
[15] I Peter 3:19-20.
[16] Luke 13:3,5.

The life in God's time and in God's way is, naturally, indescribable in wonder, beauty, peace, and power. Those who have
been caught up into heaven even here; those who have come back
feeling this present life unreal; those who have been filled with
even a bit of the Presence; those who have seen Him even from
behind, from their cleft in the rock with God's hand over them
while He passes, cannot ever describe the experience. It stuns,
it overwhelms, it is sweet unbearably, yet like a sword turned in
one's vitals; it presses the seer into a nothingness of joy. He seems
empty, not himself, cosmic. The body seems to be out of the common media of space and time. It feels transformingly light as
though made of a new substance or out of no substance at all.
One moment of such ecstasy when reached seems worth a lifetime
of suffering. Much of the rest of life becomes a longing to regain
and to retain that order of being. Yet our mountains of trans-
figuration are but the preparations of our glorification. Between
lie work and suffering. Yet the two kinds of experience are incommensurate.

This kind of ecstasy, however, may be no more than the slightest beginning of God's glory with us. "Eye hath not seen, nor ear
heard, neither have entered into the heart of man the things
which God hath prepared for them that love him."[17] That perspective, *livingly,* and that perspective *alone,* is adequate from
which to view the problem of evil. "The sufferings of this present
time are not worthy to be compared with the glory which shall
be revealed to us-ward."[18] "Our light affliction, which is for the
moment, worketh for us more and more exceedingly an eternal
weight of glory."[19] Only from the joyful anticipation, even most
dimly, of the time when the whole of God's harvest will be in
can we rightly approach the problem of evil from the perspective of truth, from the full perspective in both thought and par-

[17] I Corinthians 2:9.
[18] Romans 8:18.
[19] II Corinthians 4:17.

tial experience, of the reflexive superspective. When that stage is even beginning to be reached, in our present fragmentary lives, we experience an unrest to be done with the problem of evil as a *problem*. In that knowledge and insight of spirit, in that faith and understanding, we begin to be anxious to be done with the justifying of God either to ourselves or to others. In a state of forgiveness and faith, in a state of childlike trust, wherein we see the glory even dimly which awaits all people in God's true world, we ache to have others see and experience that new life in Christ Jesus and want more and more to do nothing so much as to render to God our gratitude for all His goodness and to glorify more fully His name, now filled with new content and meaning.

CHAPTER XIII

Points of Particular Importance

We have come to the end of this discussion. Fragmentary and merely suggestive as it is, it has nevertheless opened up, we hope, a few critical problems and cleared at least the approaches to them. There remains for others and for the future pondering of the writer to explore these further along the road ahead. What are the present trails, however, which the writer considers of particular importance?

One of these trails is surely the relation betwen the explanatory and the existential perspective on the problem of evil. Both are essential. Without knowing we cannot do; without doing we cannot know, in any adequate sense in either case. Some are interested in knowing for its own sake. These are philosophers. They speculate and try to solve the problem objectively. Yet properly speaking the problem of evil is not a philosophical one. God cannot and may not be justified by man's abstract knowledge. Explanation from man's selfish, demanding point of view that all be pleasant for him, from the point of view of his rights, is an abomination in the sight of the Lord. Neither can it be solved in terms of rational knowledge based on what is actual and merely possible in its terms.

Others there are who rightly rebel against this irresponsible or partial way of dealing with the depths of human evil, and with evil in general. Consequently they scorn all explanation. They want to overcome evil. Or they want to be judged in their own evil, repent, and leave the problem to God where they feel it to belong. Whether activists or quietists, their concern is through and through existential. Yet faith is not strong unless it also dares to see, and action is not right unless it be directed by knowledge. Neither our understanding of God nor our action can be fully calm and right unless we do obey God's command to worship Him with all our mind. Much avoidance of thinking is escapist. It is defensive. It is cowed. God has given us the light of His own glory in the face of Jesus Christ. In Him all things do indeed cohere. Though finite we are, and shall always fail of infinite knowledge, yet in that knowledge we can see more and more until the perfect day, the more we trust to Him our thinking in all areas of thought and life.

The explanatory and the existential perspectives require one another. Neither can properly speaking be said to be primary, and, at least on the subjective side, definitely not the only one. Both thinking and doing must be rooted in an event which is whole-response. For full, positive whole-living, both require each other indivisibly and completely. Each tends to become a substitute for the other. Each tends to be developed also to a great extent in opposition to the other. Such is human frailty, short in vision and weak in positive power. Being driven by our fears more than drawn by our love except as we are enclosed within the security of God's holy spirit, we actually think most forcefully, even though not most fruitfully, against some part-truth or other. When, however, we are melted together by God's love and are "perfected together in the same mind and in the same judgment"[1] we can think more faithfully along the line of God's promises and dare to explore ever new realms in order to put them under the sovereignty of the

[1] I Corinthians 1:10.

divine flag of truth. We shall get nowhere really by merely philos-
ophizing about the problem of evil. The solution can be had only
in the sanctuary of the surrendered life struggling with and under
God against evil. Nor shall we mount up with wings as eagles to
soar over the clouds of evil unless our love grows "more and more
in knowledge and all discernment."[2] The solution lies in the living
synthesis of the explanatory and the existential perspectives made
effectual only through deepened concern and trust within the
family fellowship of God.

Another point of importance is the observation that we can
never solve any problem adequately except from the full perspective of truth. We must have the fullest perspective available to
us for our central standpoint. That which cannot most fully and
meaningfully explain the origins of our process and the ends of
it; that which cannot serve as the authority, motivation, and
direction for solving our present problems and giving us now
the deepest satisfactions in struggling, having, and hoping; that
which cannot, in short, compel us most fully intellectually and
afford us the greatest practical driving power for better lives and
a better world, cannot serve as a proper standpoint from which
either to define evil or to judge whether or not the most high is,
or is not, also the most real. A partial perspective will not do.
Therefore the perspectives of mere fact, or of aesthetic satisfaction, or of present process, will not do.

Hedonism is a particularly significant perspective to watch.
Pleasure cannot serve as the fullest principle of explanation of
what ultimately is. It cannot constitute the content of our existential ultimate. It cannot be the fullest superspective of process to
account for what it is or where it points. Suffering is not, therefore,
necessarily evil. Evil must be defined by the highest purpose.
The highest purpose that we see, to effect by the Cross the
Christian fellowship, to create by self-giving love, by love suffering
for others, the kind of security and satisfaction which expresses

[2] Philippians 1:9.

itself through God and His Christ in co-operative creativeness and a free, faithful fellowship, that purpose includes intrinsically suffering. Yet only as a means. Over the Cross is the Crown.

Hedonism has a rightful truth as a secondary and subordinate perspective. It guards against a sadism and a sad-ism which take satisfaction out of the thought of suffering. Frustrated, defensive, joyless souls have a hard time to endure the thought of life and life abundantly. It seems too good to be true. They make it a point in life not to be disappointed and disillusioned on account of having too many and too high hopes. Therefore they make both God and heaven a being and condition inclusive of suffering. Salvation becomes more judgment than joy and exceeding rejoicing. They live by stern strength rather than by a happy holiness and love. Partial perspectives, however, have rightfully partial power. To disregard the partial perspective within its partial rights is also thereby to distort the fuller perspective; it is, in fact, thereby to curtail its power. Hedonism has the partial truth that suffering can be explained only as a means for fellowship within God's fuller purpose.

Purposeless suffering, therefore, is evil. We cannot tell in detail, however, what purposeless suffering is. Life is too long and too deep a process and our perspective is but a little line, or at most a few lines, out of a long story. For us to judge individual instances, seemingly irrelevant phrases, from those lines is to fail to see that the book is yet basically unread. We have a true clue to the meaning and the ending of the story. That is all. He who made the whole process with all there is in it of good and bad, from our point of view, alone knows the full story of any and all lives including their millennia of background and their illimitable future. We cannot, therefore, point to animal pain, to an idiot, or to the death of a wicked person as examples of purposeless suffering. What is in process has been made possible by God, in His wisdom, and is organically related, past, present, and future, to His fullest purpose with us and with all creatures. Our process is only a beginning. Its main nature is to point to the fuller purpose. Our own death, for instance, is no obstacle, but rather a help to explanation in terms of God. Death is within the compass and competence of Him who gives and takes life. Death is the servant, not the master, of God.

Suffering becomes purposeless only when we view it in too low a perspective. When the animal world is severed from the total purpose of God with process so as not to be included organically within the ends, animal suffering becomes purposeless. Yet such severance is on our part, not in truth. Such separation of animals or idiots from the full fact of God is the false co-ordinating of a subordinate perspective. Or again, when hell is made an eternal end for most people, or for any creature, the partial perspective of the means is raised into a co-ordinate perspective with the full perspective of God's love. There can be hell unto "the end of the ages," unto the end of our epoch, and with a divine purpose to intensify His severity over the children of disobedience that they might find for themselves the final despair of their ways and turn again home from their far country. Yet if hell is eternal as a final end the most high of God's love cannot also be fully and most powerfully and most wisely the most real. The full perspective alone gives the whole scope of truth.

At this point we must be completely careful not to confuse our explanatory and existential perspectives. There is no purposeless suffering *in the explanatory perspective* in the sense that freedom and the continual disciplining of our experience, individual and social, are altogether necessary to effect the final fellowship. Yet there is appallingly needless suffering *in the existential perspective*. Every time that we inflict harm carelessly or intentionally and every time that we fail to help the good, to relieve suffering, to break oppression, to dispel ignorance, we are guilty of adding to the world's *needless* suffering.

This is our delegated power. This is our measure of freedom. It is, of course, conditioned and controlled by God. We can, however, go the short way to the goal, as did Jesus, or take our present long route of destruction and despair.

If we stress the explanatory perspective too much we get into the torpor of the kind of absolutism against which William James protested boldly and well. If we stress the existential too much we weaken the faith in the ultimate which alone gives authority and motivation. We must stress both God and man, and in that order. Truth here as ever is a dynamic synthesis of both life and thought.

Few have written so movingly on this relation as Kierkegaard. First he stresses the primacy of life, acts, decision. Then he insists on the need for deep thought and reflection to steady life and direct decision. After a long discussion of the subject he ends thus:

> Perhaps the reflection would sometime become significant to him; it might perhaps happen that the reflection would become vividly present in his soul just when he needed it in order to penetrate the confused thoughts of his restless heart; it might perhaps happen that what the reflection had understood only in part, would sometime gather itself regenerated in the moment of decision; that what reflection had sowed in corruption would spring up in the day of need in the incorruptible life of action.[3]

As far as the question of evil goes mere reflection is corrupt. Whole-life solves the question even in the realm of truth. The explanatory perspective gives way to the existential. Yet the existential, critical as it is, must ever be superarched by the explanatory! The proper use of our freedom is essential. Yet even the use of our freedom in the fullest perspective is conditioned and controlled by God.

Yet each partial perspective has its truth within the whole scope of truth. The trick of truth is not to co-ordinate a subordinate perspective while at the same time neither to eliminate nor to minimize it. Then, too, we must never confuse that degree or

[3] Kierkegaard, *Edifying Discourses*, Vol. II, p. 13.

amount of truth that we see in the light of the reflexive super-spective, the full truth, that bit of coherence which is ours to see in our fullest synthesis of faith and reason, with the coherence which belongs to the full truth alone, to the reflexive superspective itself, else we have inadvertently confused our own seeing with the truth that we see. We have then co-ordinated our own sub-jective situation, our idea and experience of God, with God Him-self, and in fact substituted the former for the latter.

Besides the trouble with partial perspectives there is also that of mixed perspectives. A partial perspective is falsely used when it is co-ordinated in importance. It may become the principal per-spective, substituted for the true principal clause, actually sub-ordinating it. It may also be falsely co-ordinated alongside of the true co-ordinate. In that case there are not one, but two, existen-tial ultimates. There are two absolutes, infinities, two final prin-ciples of explanation. Since neither can be reduced within the compass of the other, each must limit and be limited by the other. Thus thinking may unwittingly try to operate with two or more unities of discourse in a total or inclusive sense. Consequently no adequate solution is possible. Neither partial nor mixed per-spectives can give the fully resolved chords of the composition as a whole.

Much trouble comes, for instance, when in solving the prob-lem of evil the perspective of God's love and hedonism are mixed in such a way that if God really loved us He would never have anyone suffer at any time. The perspective of God's love starts with the Cross. In that perspective we know no other God, as Luther rightly and continually insists. If we accept this per-spective at all as ultimate, we have then no right and no business to introduce as co-ordinate with it the hedonistic perspective. We must, rather, find for it its proper partial power. Though suffer-ing cannot be intruded as a co-ordinate into the ends of process, thus making its elimination as a final power and self-sufficient entity necessary to the last iota of its end-being, it must, never theless, be understood as a necessary means within the compossibles of God's being and purpose. The partial truth of hedonism is thus fulfilled, its true claim answered, its higher function absorbed within the final reality of the perfected fellowship.

Nor does this mean that the ends justify the means. Such thinking falsely severs the ends from the means. There is no adequate way of defining the means apart from the ends. When the two are defined separately and thus compared, we have a case of mixed perspectives. The real question is whether the ends are through and through worthy and whether those means are actually and truly productive of those ends. The question is not whether or not, for instance, the Cross is good as an end but whether the joy and peace in believing, whether the creative fellowship of Christian co-operation empowered and secured by God is a worthy end of history, whether history is most truly characterized by this process, and whether the Cross is in fact inclusively symbolic and conclusively effective of that end, whether the vicariousness of experience, of both suffering and sin, of both faith and grace, is the kind of means to bring about this end. As far as we can understand history and nature, they both work together to that end, in security and satisfaction as well as in insecurity and suffering. The means of history and nature, including the deepest sin and suffering and the highest redemptive triumph and salvation within them, though not sufficient for the highest eternal ends, are yet conducive to them through and through and sufficient to witness to them, and partially, indicatively, to realize them. The means and their partial realization, through their higher realizability, keep pointing through even the ends to Him who is also their Beginner.

Another aspect of our discussion which on looking back seems most important is that the compossible must be defined by God, not man. For us that means that it must be defined not in terms of human speculation about what ought to be according to our wants as we now actually and generally are, but rather in terms of truth's historic concretion. The determinative truth must be incarnational, embodied, become flesh. The reflexive superspec-tive must not be arrived at through idle fancy or "a detached logic," usually of the natural man, but rather through the selective actual, through the point of the arrow which best shows where the process as a whole is going, through the selective ideal which most fully explains the nature and direction of the process as a whole, *through a solid rather than through a hollow standard of truth.*

To say, for instance, that God should be able to produce and should want to produce the fruits of the Cross without it, the warmth of fellowship hallowed by suffering and sacrifice and through a common struggle without these experiences, the grati-tude of grace without the need for forgiveness, the richness of creative growth without any difficulties to overcome—to say such things is idle fancy. In the explanatory perspective it is thin part-thinking, speculative daydreaming. In the existential perspective it may be escapist, the refusal to accept the Cross as the wisdom and power of God's love. The Christian compossible is defined by the Cross, with respect to means, and by God Himself as Agape with respect to ends. For us those ends require those means. The Agape whom we know is always against the back-ground of the law and sin. He is the Agape of the Cross. He is known not as love in general, however generous, but conclusively and exclusively as the Love of the Cross who conquers death and sets us free from sin and from death. Nothing less than the God of the Cross in all His goodness and severity is the God of truth. The compossible grace *on the level of creation* must not minimize but must enrich this redemptive truth. Here Luther is completely correct:

> Wherefore when thy Conscience standeth in the conflict, wrestling against the Law, Sin and Death, in the Presence of God, there is nothing more dangerous than to wander with curious Speculations in Heaven, and there to search out God in his in-

comprehensible Power, Wisdom and Majesty, how he created the
World, and how he governeth it. . . . But out of the matter of
Justification, when thou must dispute . . . concerning the Power,
Wisdom and Majesty of God, then employ all thy Wit and In-
dustry to that End, and be as profound and subtle a Disputer as
thou canst; for then thou art in another Vein.[4]

When we are dealing with the means of salvation, the process
of perfecting and making effectual the Christian fellowship, the
compossible must be solidly defined in terms of the highest, most
conclusive, and most inclusive symbol, the life, teachings, and
Cross of Christ. Any idle speculation here is out of the focus of
rewarding truth, truth organically operative within our sinful
actual world.

That the present tense of process alone is real naturally has a
crucial bearing on our problem. If the past as past remained real,
an unalterable part of every present, the means would always
remain within the ends. The past, however, is constantly being
canceled out by each present. In nature there is a continual process of neutralization going on. The processes of nature seem to
exhibit a rhythm of restoration which is somewhat proportionate
to the grade of life. This whole question, from the inorganic
level through unicellular life through multicellular and highly
developed organism, must wait for an adequate investigation and
discussion until we deal in a future volume, we hope, with the
whole question of nature. The problem of the relation of mind
and body is peculiarly fascinating in this respect.

When we reach human experience, however, particularly, the
spiritual kernel of it, we arrive at the possibility of abrupt and
radical discontinuity. We find that experience is through and
through transmutable. The traitor may become the loyal fol-
lower; the persecutor, the apostle; the recanter, the martyr. The
past can become different even as its meaning is modified and
transmuted by a present meaning. Even God does not have to

[4] *Op. cit.*, pp. 33-34.

be tortured by the memory of the past that is no more when it is truly forgiven and also canceled out in nature, in this world or through death, or through whatever processes in a future life. God not only forgives, but He forgets our sins. When we forgive and forget, God does, too. We can forgive because He is ever willing to forgive us and to give us the power to be like Him. That the present tense of process alone is real, containing within it all pasts of process, either already having their evils canceled out or having them ready within each present for cancellation has, accordingly, direct and heavy bearing on the problem of evil.

This personal-spiritual level, furthermore, seen most truly in the selective actual and ideal, must ever be kept as the level of our interpretation. The very center of the perspective, of course, must be that selective actual and ideal, namely, Jesus Christ as the revealer and effector in human history, decisively, of God's Agape-fellowship. Yet the problems not on this level of interpretation are genuine problems of *knowledge* and must be related as well as possible to our central perspective. The sorest problems that we struck were those on the animal level and the divine, on the levels below and above the human. Such speculative thinking as we have extended to those levels may debilitate faith. Perhaps we have no right and no business to concern ourselves with these questions. They should perhaps be put beyond the limits of faith. The fideists may have a real point here. The problems of animal pain and of divine suffering are, however, our two outstanding problems. The reason that we have discussed them is that we believe that faith can see more truly than fear, the higher than the lower perspective.

We admit freely that we cannot ccmpellingly explain animal pain, for instance, but the truth as a whole of God and of His way with men is so powerful that we can leave in His hands, without evasion, that problem. We have nevertheless essayed attempts at solution which in the larger perspective of process as a whole, put up against God's patient and painstaking way of working—his long process, as we see it, and yet blitz-short in eternity—may be suggestive, relating the evolution of body to the evolution of soul, the evolution of nature to the evolution of history. Perhaps in this cosmos this process is even now merely beginning and mankind may right now be standing on the eve of another stage in its development and plenary power.

God's suffering also remains a problem. It is with us much of a mystery. It is the central mystery of the Incarnation. That the eternal joy and fulness of being comes down to take on our infirmities and sorrows, as Luther says, such things "mightily fight against Reason."[5] Yet we must start there. Else we cannot get at the highest perspective of truth. The reason that this idea fights so hard against reason is that our reason is limited to the confines of process. God's full Agape-love is here hard to see even according to our measure and that alone makes such humiliation possible. We can see eternity, furthermore, only through the inverted parentheses of time. We must draw "the limits of faith." This is part of our existential situation. God's full Agape-love is mostly a mystery because we cannot fathom the eternity which is beyond our kind of time. We think only within the categories of our kinds of experience. How narrow those categories must be! How some day we shall wonder at their strait limits. The mystery of God's suffering is basically due to our idea that to be love He must ever create. Yet this need not be so, since perfection lacks nothing and since the divine fellowship can be eternally rich within itself. If we try to rest in that position, however, we are up against the arbitrariness of this creation, of our little time. Without repeating the many ins and outs of this problem we can say that we find most intellectual satisfaction in the classic solution that God suffers in history only. Yet existentially God's suffering is essential to our understanding of His love. We must have a savior who suffers with us, if He is to be love, fully and freely; at least we long for such a one. There is no problem about that. The weak-

[5] *Op. cit.*, p. 212.

nesses of nature are God's humility for our sake. There is no evil there with which He cannot identify Himself. And surely Love identifies Himself with His own children in their trying to go their own way until they find that the Father's way is the best even for them.

The only problem that we have on this score is whether the Father suffers, whether suffering is an aspect of eternity as well as time. The mystery is indeed of *the divine condescension into history* and how such suffering can be there without being also in eternity. The mystery is, while there is one God, how the Son can suffer and not the Father. Existentially the need for a suffering savior is so utterly pressing that we can see how men turn from God to Jesus and to Mary because they can understand our weaknesses, sufferings, and sorrows. Jesus then becomes, however, a substitute for God rather than the mediator. He is no longer a door to pass through. He may thus hinder rather than help our full knowledge of God. If Jesus becomes too closely identified with God, men may turn to Mary.

Does this not mean that in all these realms, in these "veins," we must, as Luther warns us, have a completely Christ-centered God, that God must be known through and through in terms of the selective actual and ideal? At this point, however, we must honestly admit that our whole-response does not completely include whole-thinking. There is a paradox in this ultimate relation which demands faith crucially beyond what we can see. Agape must suffer with all sufferers. Yet if God must create always, being Agape, and must therefore always suffer with His creation, what right does He have, or how can He, being Agape, share His suffering with new creatures whom He invites to accept the Cross? Experience shows us that love is peace and joy—even in suffering—and overcomes suffering. Perhaps we must glue our minds and hearts to the actual experience of God in Christ, on His love and beyond our fullest experience, and forsake the peripheral problems of joy and suffering as not relevant to our stature now as creatures of earth with dust in our eyes, nearly closing them.

We must think as men in history, as creatures, and as sinners, whether unforgiven or forgiven, not as God or as saints in glory. Though the truth opened by the light of God's Incarnation illumines history most fully, explaining it better than any other standpoint, that truth itself as it opens up onto eternity is man's basic mystery. Beyond our seeing we must gaze, and gazing we must gratefully adore. The wisdom and power of God we acknowledge and have known confirmingly in both our thought and experience. Yet that wisdom and power are far beyond our ideas of them. Our ideas end in that blazing light and glory which make them seem thin and empty. See we must. Yet mere seeing, however much, cannot save. Salvation from evil, even from the evil of limited sight, is possible only through whole-surrender. It is possible only through faith, grace, and grateful obedience.

In the end, therefore, those are certainly right who have understood that our basic approach to the problem of evil is not to justify God, but to have Him judge and justify us. Our seeing must begin and end in faith. Our seeing is through whole-response to God. We see as saved sinners. We see as sons restored through love to the family fellowship. This our seeing we can share with all who have had our experience and with all who are ready to surrender their inadequate spiritual defenses. Beyond that we cannot go.

Sovereignty in seeing belongs to the spirit. Who knows the spirit of man except man or the spirit of God except through the Spirit?[6] Our reason, however, can be used by the Holy Spirit to convict us of either ignorance or willful distortion. The Holy Spirit can work through truth in all men and any, in order to light each and all who come into the world, both convicting them of darkness and of sin, and offering them peace and pardon, security and satisfaction, freedom, fellowship, and creative joy *in God.*

[6] Cf. I Corinthians 2:11.

There are problems in holding that whole-response can be whole-seeing. In the end we must rest with the fact that though religious seeing is our fullest possible seeing, and is completely necessary to the fullest faith, the fullest faith, nevertheless, outstrips it immeasurably in content, and raises besides a final qualitative barrier of mystery, God inhabiting eternity while we live in created time, making us live immeasurably more by God's power than by our own seeing.

Reason in the Christian faith is sufficient to show us that the most high is also the most real—if we will but see. Such seeing, however, comes only with clinching grace through surrender to the claims of God's love and holy living. All that we have and are must be put in His service. When that is done, our reason becomes no theory without power to serve and to save. It becomes, rather, an instrument in God's hand whereby our understanding obedience constitutes a channel of God's mercy and an aid in the overcoming of evil. Reason in the Christian faith is then no false comfort for the selfishly insecure, but the challenge of faith for a needy world. The explanatory perspective becomes an aid to the existential and the existential to the explanatory. In a world like this, to which we now turn our practical attention in the volume to follow, we need knowledge through the light of life, but also knowledge for our life in the light.

The Christian Faith

Our concern here is with the heart of the Christian faith. The purpose of this appendix is to suggest, as a working hypothesis only, the governing meaning and reality of the Gospel. What we are after is to give a concrete content to the most high in order to be able to use this as a principle for explaining the nature of evil and to indicate the manner of and resources for its solution.

The Christian faith will necessarily be tested by its capacity to answer in thought and deed, in truth and action, this central problem of religion. Only if the content of our faith can be judged in the balance of the world's needs and not found wanting has it a right to be the judge and saviour of the world. Naturally we cannot, and should not, give more here than the regulative pattern and determinative reality, the governing presupposition, of the Christian faith. That heart of the faith, however, must be sufficiently defined to help explain most fully both our intellectual problems and our practical needs, besides indicating and making available the authority and motivation actually to solve them.

The definition of the Christian faith which we have previously expounded at length is to the effect that Christianity is the freedom and faithfulness in fellowship, grounded in God and empowered by Him, which is based on the kind of love, God's own self, God's holy Agape, which was first fully revealed as central in cosmos and conduct, i.e., in ultimate reality and as a standard for conduct, and made effective in history by Jesus Christ. This thought has been enlarged upon in three volumes: *The Christian Fellowship, The Christian Faith,* and *Return to Christianity.*

Here certain aspects of this must be made emphatic. What we want to stress is that Jesus dominantly both was and taught Agape for the first time in human history. Agape[1] is the kind of love which God is, which received conclusive expression in Jesus, and which lives ever as the central and controlling reality wherever there is genuine Christian fellowship. This appendix is written particularly to enlarge on our understanding of what Agape is and what it means when related to human actions, standards, and meanings.

Before presenting these definitions, let us repeat that nowhere else than in Christ did Agape become first fully central both as to the interpretation of God and as to man's relation with man. This is a historic fact. It is not, however, a fact for invidious comparison. The more Agape can be found elsewhere and previously, the better.

Jesus is distinctive of Christian faith. He is distinctive precisely because he both lived and taught this reality. He is history's Most High. He is the Word become flesh, full of grace and truth. No incarnation of Agape or full teaching of it in any real sense at all is to be found in Greek thought. "The Greek mind never reached the conception of a divine love for man as man" and "in the contemporary cults no evidence is to be found for such

---

[1] Naturally what matters is in no significant way the word but the reality which the word conveys. A wise professor in Upsala long ago warned the writer not to press the word, especially historically. What we are after all centers in the nature and the purpose of God. Even sinners have Agape *as far as the word goes*! (Cf. Luke 6:32.)

Although all Agape is ultimately from God, we use the word impersonally to avoid pantheistic language. This is not altogether satisfactory because some may conclude that we think of Agape as a self-sufficient structure apart from the concurrent activity of God. We want neither pantheistic nor deistic language, but we know no language that is thoroughly theistic. The primacy incomparably is obviously God's; yet man's secondary response to it and appropriation of it is also fully real.

divine love."[2] "On examination, the analogy between Platonic and Christian love is revealed as nothing more than superficial."[3]

Paul Minear suggests that Jesus be called God's love enacted. That is precisely our meaning. The message which he was alone explains the message which he taught. This enacted message, moreover, is never to be found in a universal sense in Judaism. Who can read Hosea and the author of Jonah and not feel vibrant within their lives and messages anticipations of Jesus? Who can read the great passages in the Prophet of the Exile without seeing their messages fulfilled in Jesus? We want to see in the Old Testament all the Agape that we can. Yet undoubtedly Snaith is right when he says that the highest pinnacle of that great religious revelation was God's election-love and covenant love.[4] Yahweh's love was basically confined to His chosen people.

Not in Judaism, before Jesus, was there any dominant enactment in life and thought that God is Agape so that all else is to be seen in this light. Montefiore's statement is conclusive to the effect that in the Old Testament there is "no emergence of love as the one great supreme link between man and God, as at once the essence of the divine nature and the ideal of all human nature."[5] Thus in spite of the deep and binding continuity between Judaism and Christianity Agape is the conclusive discontinuity which makes Christianity what it is. In a way we might say that Jesus universalized the deepest in Judaism: "The most important of all the distinctive ideas of the Old Testament is God's steady and extraordinary persistence in continuing to love wayward Israel in spite of Israel's insistent waywardness."[6] According to the Agape which Jesus was and taught, God is now seen to love all.[7]

---

[2] Moffat, *Love in the New Testament*, p. 10.

[3] Cochrane, *Christianity and Classical Culture*, p. 502.

[4] Snaith, *The Distinctive Ideas of the Old Testament*.

[5] Montefiore, *The Old Testament and After*, p. 209.

[6] Snaith, *op. cit.*, p. 102.

[7] Even to this full position there are certainly important approaches in the Old Testament as in the books of Ruth and Jonah, Leviticus 19, etc.

Champion, in *The Eleven Religions*, suggests that love is the pinnacle of all the great religions. Yet in spite of all the great ethical insights in Mencius, Analects, Tao Tê Ching, Bhagavad-Gita, Dhammapada, etc., and all the other great, pre-Christian religious classics, the writer knows of no passage in which a personal God of Agape is made supreme ultimately and where the complete losing of oneself into this fellowship and for and with one another is made the standard for all human conduct. The question is not one of superiority but of fact. The more Agape that can be found outside Christianity the better, for that merely increases the early manifoldness of God's revelation. The question is not primarily one of finding self-sacrifice but of finding in these writings the nature of God and what He requires of us, or more deeply, offers to us. The full picture of that is not to be found in any pre-Christian religion.

This understanding of God as Agape which was conclusively revealed in life and light through Jesus is not only the distinctive but also the determinative meaning and reality of the Christian faith. In our previous writings we have made much of the Synoptic tradition. There the central parables of the Prodigal Son, the Good Samaritan, the Laborers in the Vineyard, etc. stress this central message. There we are bidden to be perfect even as our Father who is good to the unthankful and the evil. There we are bidden to love our enemies and to do good without question of reward, in order that we might have the true reward of being members of the heavenly Kingdom.

The disciples of Christ must forgive endlessly. The Golden Rule fulfills the law and the prophets, but it is certainly not the Christian Gospel. The law and the prophets were until John, but now the least of the Kingdom is greater than the best under the old order. Something revolutionarily new has come into history, radically changing the view of God and His relation with men and their relation with one another. All mutuality is done away as a basis for right relationship. We must love the Lord our God with all our heart, strength, and mind, and our neighbor as ourself. The natural man loves himself first. There is no problem about that. The disciples, however, must love God and others the way the natural man loves himself—*first*! Here is surely no justification of self-love. Only in the context of the first commandment does the second have the right meaning; then love to self comes to mean to be lost completely in love for God and others, and is, in effect, abolished.

In addition to the direct teaching of Agape, moreover, one of Jesus' clearest ways of teaching it is indirect; for instance, his teaching of complete trust in God. Jesus stressed faith in God over and over again—complete, utter faith. Now, faith, as Brunner maintains with unerring insight, "is nothing but the affirmation of love."[8] The God whom you can trust completely with every detail of your life, the God who cares for every sparrow on the tree, the God who clothes each lily in the field, that God is a Father with an utterly dependable fatherly presence and care. Jesus' healing ministry was built on the assumption that God cared completely for us if we only had faith enough to let Him help us. This constant stress on how much God cares and how He can do all things seems nearly insane to us. It surely seems absurd, irrational. Did Jesus not see how evil the world was? How, then, could he say what he did and really believe as he did? That God is love who can be perfectly trusted is not an easy inference from the experience of our lives and our histories. It is rather incredible to the ordinary life and thinker.

Usually the best way to find out what a person really believes is by watching his almost unconscious assumptions and presuppositions, those things which he seems to take for granted which lie deeper than discursive thought. The basic presupposition of Jesus' life in both teaching and living, in helping and healing, in success and in apparent defeat was that God, his Father, could

[8] Brunner, *God and Man*, p. 121.

be trusted perfectly. Faith in the wisdom and power of God's love is the inner spring of Jesus' life. And his teachings everywhere punctuate this basic attitude and understanding.

Before the Synoptic Gospels came to be written were the writings of Paul. With him the greatest of the things which remained was the divine Agape.[9] Elton Trueblood has observed that Paul had to use a whole chapter to define Agape—and more than a chapter.[10] Love is the fulfillment of the law.[11] God commends His own love to us, in that, while we were yet sinners, Christ died for us.[12] Those who would imitate Paul, as he did Christ, must not seek their own profit but the profit of the many.[13] All were members of the same body and should have the same care for one another.[14] Paul's whole life in the flesh was one of faith in the Son of God who loved him and gave himself up for him.[15] Nothing is of any avail except faith working through love.[16]

Freedom is to be found only as in love we become servants of one another.[17] To be followers of Christ is to be ambassadors of reconciliation between God and men, God taking the initiative, freely forgiving,[18] to be constrained by the love of Christ.[19] The law of Christ is to bear one another's burdens.[20] We must know the love of Christ which goes beyond knowledge in order to be filled unto all the fullness of God.[21] The unity of the faith, and of the knowledge of the Son of God, the very measure of the

[9] Cf. I Corinthians 13:13.
[10] Trueblood, *Foundations for Reconstruction*, p. 108.
[11] Cf. Romans 13:10; Galatians 5:14.
[12] Cf. Romans 5:8.
[13] Cf. I Corinthians 11:1; 10:33.
[14] Cf. I Corinthians 12:27,25.
[15] Cf. Galatians 2:20.
[16] Cf. Galatians 5:6.
[17] Cf. Galatians 5:13.
[18] Cf. II Corinthians 5:18-20.
[19] Cf. II Corinthians 5:14.
[20] Cf. Galatians 6:2.
[21] Cf. Ephesians 3:19.

stature of the fullness of Christ, can come only as the body grows up, as it builds up in love.[22]

To imitate God as beloved children we must walk in love even as Christ also loved us and gave himself up for us.[23] Love must abound more and more in knowledge and all discernment.[24] The mind of Christ is the humble self-giving love which goes to the Cross.[25] Our hearts must be knit together in love that we may have all the riches of the full assurance of understanding and may know the mystery of God, even Christ, in whom all the treasures of wisdom and knowledge are hidden.[26] Above all things, Paul, or the Pauline author, stresses, we must put on love which is the bond of perfectness.[27] There is no need even to write concerning love of the brethren for we are taught of God to love one another.[28] Every good work and word comes from the Father who loved us and gave us eternal comfort and good hope through grace.[29] *This is the Pauline stress throughout,* whether or not Paul actually wrote all these epistles: our salvation must be based through faith on God's free love as shown and made effective in Christ Jesus. Here alone is full freedom from sin, the law, and death. The passages where the divine Agape is explicitly mentioned, moreover, are also strongly backed by that great stress in Pauline literature on God's grace and that freedom which comes only when, beyond the law, we understand and accept the very heart and purpose of God.

Of the Johannine literature it is almost unnecessary to write. There God is defined as love with passionate insistence. We can hardly say, nevertheless, that it is more so than in Paul, who

[22] Cf. Ephesians 4:12-16.
[23] Cf. Ephesians 5:1-2.
[24] Cf. Philippians 1:9.
[25] Cf. Philippians 2:1-8.
[26] Cf. Colossians 2:2-3.
[27] Cf. Colossians 3:14.
[28] Cf. I Thessalonians 4:9.
[29] II Thessalonians 2:16.

presupposes and works throughout with God's good gift of grace in Christ Jesus. Paul, for instance, has the chapter on the divine love as the fulfillment of ethics which can hardly be surpassed. Yet there are in the Johannine literature certain passages which add much to the basic unity of the New Testament.

"Hereby know we love, because he laid down his life for us: and we ought to lay down our lives for the brethren."[30] The commandment is that we should believe in the name of Jesus Christ His Son and love one another. "We love, because he first loved us."[31] "Beloved, let us love one another: for love is of God; and everyone that loveth is begotten of God, and knoweth God . . . for God is love. Herein was the love of God manifested in us, that God hath sent his only begotten Son into the world that we might live through him. Herein is love, not that we love God, but that he loved us, and sent his Son to be the propitiation for our sins. Beloved, if God so loved us, we ought to love one another."[32] "Whosoever believeth that Jesus is the Christ is begotten of God: and whosoever loveth him that begat loveth him also that is begotten of him. Hereby we know that we love the children of God, when we love God and do his commandments."[33] To those who love God these commandments are not grievous. They are a joy that overcomes the world through its faith. "Perfect love casteth out fear."[34] "For God so loved the world that he gave his only begotten Son that whosoever believeth in him should not perish but have eternal life."[35] This is the great Gospel of the Johannine literature.

There is a strong, all-pervading unity in the New Testament. Minor strands and minor stresses do exist. But the melody is clear and open to those who will hear. To the writer, the New Testa-

[30] I John 3:16.
[31] I John 4:19.
[32] I John 4:7-11.
[33] I John 5:12.
[34] I John 4:18.
[35] John 3:16.

ment is a great miracle. What creative power, what rich insights, what fullness of truth! Never could this have been written, it seems, so unmistakably centered as it is around one person, unless that person had both been and taught, with a dominant force beyond our imagination, the centrality of the divine love.

The unity of the New Testament is not, however, the teaching of love, even of God's love. Here is no philosophy either of reality or of life in a speculative sense. The unity is through and through centered in a person. The New Testament is essentially biographical. Here is history's most high. Here is the determinative, selective actual. Here is realizability and realization. Here is truth exemplified in life. We often hear about the religion *of* Jesus as over against the religion *about* Jesus. The two are supposed to be radically different. On the very contrary, they must necessarily go together. The religion of Jesus was God's love which possessed him and worked in him. The religion about Jesus is God's love which possessed him and worked through him.

Jesus is the decisive historic instance. Here heaven and earth meet. When they meet what matters most to earth is heaven; and to heaven, earth. *God* became human; God became *human.* The Word became flesh. The Word of God is principally not a book, nor a law, nor a theory, but a life. The religion of the New Testament is not a perversion of Jesus' Gospel. It is the Gospel. He is the Gospel. That is the Word to be preached instantly in and out of season. He revealed and made effective in history the Begetter, his own Source and Power. How can we love Him who begat without loving the first-born among many brethren, him who was begotten, the reality of God's love in history, its concrete embodiment in truth and grace?

In order to make our understanding of Agape still more clear, we venture the following definitions. Agape is a synthesis of meaning and mystery. To confine it within our definitions, therefore, is to forget that *God* is Agape. He is sovereign in reality and function, in action and being, far beyond our best thought. Our knowledge is ever, as St. Thomas Aquinas well reminds us, according to the mode of the knower.[36] We can never know God except as He has made it possible for us and has made Himself known to us. Beyond is mystery.

Yet not to define Him is to substitute vagueness for clarity, confusion for order, the contradictions of our own muddled minds for His revealed clarity. Christianity is *the religion of revelation*, not of mystery. It is not a mystery cult. It is the religion of Incarnation, not of the unknown or of the hidden God. It is what Ignatius calls "a thing of (manifest) greatness,"[37] and this refers to its truth as well as its deed. The more we meditate in the Holy Spirit on the meaning of God, the better it is; the more we are filled with His riches; the deeper and fuller the vision becomes. Nervous activism needs the quiet, growing power of contemplation, of the worship of God with all our minds. This, of course, must go along with worship and action, without both of which the essence of religion is denied. Yet the danger of academic abstraction is also close at hand, crouching behind every student's chair. For that reason we approach our task of trying to indicate the richness of Agape with fear and trembling as well as with joy and confidence, with the truth firmly in mind that He is the synthesis of the fullest meaning and the deepest mystery. Only in this way shall we succeed.

1. *God* is Agape. That is ever first and primary. Agape, in one sense, is not God. Ultimate is not a principle but a Person. Agape is the nature of Perfect Spirit, the character of the Ideal Person. It is the basic meaning of God's activity. It is primarily divine, not human, love. It is the content of the Purpose of this process and of all processes.

---

[36] *Summa Theologica*, I, 12.4.
[37] "Epistle of Ignatius to the Romans," in *Ante-Nicene Fathers*, Vol. I, p. 75. Cf. also St. Athanasius, *The Incarnation of the Word of God* (Centenary Press, 1944), pp. 90 ff.

Agape is basically *He*, and only secondarily *it*. When Agape is used impersonally, as above *passim*, it is used to describe the way God works, or lets work. This use is always false and misleading if it is taken to mean that God is not its ultimate source. It is easy to slide from the Person to the process as ultimate. While Agape and God are synonymous, they are not readily interchangeable in word order; but that is for our sake. Since we can abstract the work from the Worker, the creation from the Creator, nature from being, we must stress that *God* is Agape.

The central being and activity of God is Agape and all Agape is from and of Him. Obviously the created order and most of our human willing operate on the basis of Eros, desiring "love," but even this operation is purposed by God's Agape in order to produce finally a real fellowship of Agape. Agape is the final being, nature, purpose, and function of God. All else is the effect or the function, primarily or secondarily, of what He is. God *is Agape*.

2. Agape is also our final principle of explanation. Truth is through and through God-centered. That which is not God or of God, yet must owe its possibility of existence to Him and to His activity. In the main section we have shown how this particularly affects our understanding of evil. All non-being and partial being, the mixture of being and non-being, of being and becoming, of reality with possibility, must in the end, directly and indirectly, be referable to God. Truth is God-centered, even the truth of our process and all processes, making Agape our final and all-embracing principle of explanation.

3. Agape is holy. God is absolutely holy. Holiness is the very nature of Agape. His nature is always to remain Himself, entirely pure. Holiness is the intrinsic self-consistency of Agape whereby He never becomes contaminated by any evil, never defiled by any corruption, never even tempted by any uncleanness. To the Pure all things are pure for they are external to Him and incapable of in the least way entering into Him. Holiness is the wholeness of Agape.

To us this means separation from God except on His own basis. It means that we separate ourselves from Him by our rebellion. He does not separate Himself from us; rather He seeks us. His holiness seeks holiness in us. His deepest longing is to give His holiness to us, His own purity, His own Agape. This can be done only as we are forgiven, forsake that which is evil, forego that inner self-seeking from which flow out all the basic evils of the world.

Only as by faith we accept God's Agape can we become holy, be made whole, be restored to fellowship, escape our separation from God.

In the main section we discuss why sovereign holiness should create this kind of world and how such creation can be consistent with that holiness. Nothing must in any way, however, minimize in the slightest that Agape is altogether holy. For us there can be no individual or social salvation except on the basis of holiness, of our having been made whole together, purified of all evil desire. None can truly love his fellow man except through the *Holy* Spirit. Agape is holy. Without this stress we have human, sentimental love. Agape is the Holy Spirit.

That Agape is perfectly holy means that He is perfectly just. Agape never abrogates justice. He redeems it. The justice of God depends upon a finally right order of things, upon the righteous and effective administration of a perfect law. Agape never weakens the final rightness of things. Agape makes it possible, rather, to attain that rightness by His own power of forgiveness, conversion, and restoration. Agape takes upon Himself in history the consequences of our sins and pays for them, then makes a new order of things possible by a new light and a new power of life. Thus sin is actually always paid for by suffering, by God's suffering, Agape's suffering, in Christ and in all the saints who fulfill his sufferings.

The rightness of things is respected. God is utterly holy. Yet the law is not only condemnatory; justice is not only a matter of equity, but beyond, the law and justice are reclamatory and re-habilitory. Agape fulfills the law. He fulfills justice. He makes a new order possible where the rightness of things is possible and effective. The law becomes written and fulfilled in each man's heart in the God-centered fellowship reality.

The outer compulsion becomes inner spontaneity. God's order becomes our freedom, His command our wish. Agape is the fulfillment of both justice and law. All justice and law point to Agape. They are pedagogical in His service. He is their end and direction. Agape is the locus of the law's fulfillment. Agape is thus in every way perfectly holy. Without this stress there is no *divine* love.

4. Agape is active love. The attitude and the action are one. It is faith completed by works. The action can be separate from the attitude in us only because of our finitude. In God they go together perfectly. In us, however, there is no Agape that does not result in action up to the maximum limit of our capacity. The attitude issues by its very nature in action. Even these verbs, "result," "issues," are prejudicial. They presuppose an isolated being, contemplating, feeling sympathy, and perhaps helping. That is not Agape.

Agape cannot pass by on the other side. To have it is to help. How can we love God and shut up our hearts to human needs? The problem of Agape is always where to act and how, where and why to stop from any action. Jesus leaves those seeking healing in order to find solitude and power in prayer, to commune with God. That is the very presupposition of life. Communion in Agape-love is central. Fellowship is first. That is life's chief end. That is God's own purpose with creation. Yet that Agape the next moment will leave the ninety and nine to seek the one lost, the one in need of help.

There is no completely rational rule by which one can judge when to commune with God and when to help, or how much. We must not estimate our action so seriously that we fail to make the one Agape-action central in history. Waiting on Him in prayer might produce deeper and more helping action than our hurried help, however well meant. The only rule is that we must know the true worshipers by their fruit. No attitude, nevertheless, is ever authentic Agape unless it be the central spring of one's being which issues inevitably in action.

Few people have ever written more understandingly of active love than Dostoievsky in *The Brothers Karamazov*. He holds this aspect of it to be a key to its understanding. Those whose faith is slipping can regain it in this way only. A review of Brunner's *Justice and the Social Order* in *Svensk teologisk kvartalskrift*[38] complains that Brunner differs from the Swedish understanding of Christian love by separating the attitude from the action. Agape is love in action. Redemptive justice is the inner soul of Agape at work in a sinful world. That action might, however, the writer feels very strongly, often be a refusal to participate in efforts at justice which will be self-defeating because inadequate in motivation and approach.

The Cross is also action; it is, indeed, the central action of God in history. Agape is action aimed always at the fullest redemption and highest reclamatory justice. Alternate courses of action from those generally accepted often are Agape's way. His way is generally selective, for the few. His action is the morality which is "love irradiated by reason.[39]

Agape is God at work in the world. My Father works. "Love is not merely an outward mark and symbol of His presence but is His very self at work in our world."[40] Agape is active love where according to capacity the attitude and the action are one. God alone is ever full Agape in this sense of power and perfection. All infinite union of attitude and action is ever at best a matter of "relative perfection."

[38] January, 1946, by Gösta Hök.
[39] Cochrane, *Christianity and Classical Culture*, p. 506.
[40] Baillie, *The Interpretation of Religion*, p. 470.

5. Agape, furthermore, is perfect wisdom. Agape is the full use of the mind for all and for the truth in everything. Agape is wisdom at work. It is God's truth, or God as truth, at work. It is "reason irradiated by love."[41] Agape is the loving of God, all, and everything with all our mind. Agape is fully logical, consistent with Himself, with *itself* when seen partially, yet then ever only fully and truly so when rightly related to Him who is Agape. The Holy Spirit is the spirit of truth. Since the Holy Spirit is Agape "in spiritual matters certitude belongs not to reason but to love. Our conviction goes only so deep as our love."[42]

"Knowledge puffeth up, but love edifieth. . . . If any man loveth God, the same is known by him."[43] "Hence he who possesses the more charity, will see God the more perfectly."[44] Only the love of the truth can save for truth is love. Agape is the truth. The truth is Agape. Our fullest dedication to truth is the work of Agape. In whatever field of work we are in, complete intellectual honesty with ourselves and with our work is of God.

6. Agape, again, is perfect power. He is power at work according to His perfect purpose. Agape is all the power there is. This power is the full capacity to control and to condition all and everything. It is the ability inclusively to direct all and everything. Agape shares its power, delegates it, yet not irresponsibly. Such delegated power is ever conditioned and controlled for the sake of the objects of His love. Agape has the power of patience to let others make mistakes, rebel against Him for the sake of finding for themselves freely and fully the truth that truly saves and satisfies and makes secure. Agape has the humility of power to endure rejection and rebellion even of Himself and His best goal for all until those who possess the delegated power learn and accept His meaning. Both pedagogically and finally Agape is

[41] Cochrane, *op. cit.*
[42] Dickie, *Revelation and Response,* p. 67.
[43] I Corinthians 8:1-2.
[44] Thomas Aquinas, *Summa Theologica,* I, 12, 7.

perfect power. Wherever Agape is truly proclaimed, power is, therefore, present. "Not only is a word spoken, but something *happens.*"[45]

7. Agape, besides, is perfect freedom. That they have this and that they can then use it according to the needs of their natures to find the truth through trial and error, through rebellions and returns, is no limitation on God. He wants it. He does not want men to sin, but He wants them to become understanding, willing, and loving children through the experience of freedom. That this freedom be, and be used, is according to His own purpose. This includes man's standing aside from God to question Him, standing over against Him in order to understand Him freely, in order to learn to serve Him freely, and in order to learn to love Him freely.

Here we see why God gave us Eros, a desiring love centering dominantly in self. Eros is part of the pedagogical purpose of God. We pervert it by sin. Eros finds frustration in self, fulfillment in God, tragedy in "my will," peace and power in "not my will but thine." All of man's spiritual history is centered in this contrast, which is given with intent by God.

God alone is perfectly free with the freedom of full Agape. We become free to whatever extent we accept Agape. In Agape the Cross is willingly accepted. There is no limitation on us from without or within to whatever extent we live according to God's purpose for then all things work out for the best for us and for all men. God alone being perfectly free, no human being has the freedom to resist God except within the limits of His delegated power. God has given to each man a measure of freedom within His sovereign control, else were neither man nor God finally free. Because God is sovereign in His free purpose His severity and goodness are both adequate to lead man to repentance, and the gifts and promises of God are not repented of. His free faithfulness is ever more mighty than our conditioned and controlled

[45] Nygren, *Romarbrevet,* p. 75, translation mine.

faithlessness, for He cannot deny Himself. Because both God and man have freedom there is no predetermined history possible. Only God's own end with history according to His own nature and purpose is predetermined.

Kirk points out in a beautiful passage, furthermore, that love confers independence on its object, that it also frees the giver, makes him objective, and that being of God it is irresistible in His time and way.[46] To love is to bestow freedom on the other, make him an end. Because God loves perfectly He bestows on us the maximum freedom consistent with our best possible end. Agape is perfectly free. Can we say that Agape confers the maximum freedom on each and all for each and all, for and with each other, and for what each one most deeply craves according to the very constitution of his nature? God's love thus confers in this way, and by means of the control of man's environment, a freedom within the conditions and controls of his own sovereign will for a perfectly good and worthy end. Thus love knows no limits to its freedom.

8. What more shall we say? To define Agape is to describe all that is good. He is the source of all. Agape is responsible concern rooted in response to God's love. It is what Brunner calls responding to "generous love with responsive love."[47] It is unconditional love. Love never fails. Love forgives seventy times seventy as the small start of a long process. The conditions of love are not lack of concern, if authentic love be there, God in us, but matters of wisdom of action or relation.

Divine love is our identification with others unto the utmost of our capacity and God's full identification with all for their best, redemptively. We identify ourselves with the world's sins and sufferings, ignorance and folly, but more with the cleansing power of God's love and holiness which works in us. We become sin beyond ourselves with the world to God but also righteousness

[46] *The Vision of God*, pp. 343 ff.
[47] Brunner, *Man in Revolt*, p. 485.

and redemption from God to the world. Agape is uncalculating in seeking not its own. It is gratitude to God for all His goodness. It is the fountain of all joy welling up everlastingly.

9. Agape is also perfect beauty. Beauty reveals the nature of God. It also makes us joint creators with Him. God was good to give us art. Art is for us a bridge to Agape, to His own self. It makes us want to share over and above all selfish possession or interest. Mixed motives may also be present but they are not the heart of true art, or the love of art. Creative art is the feel of the pulse of God within the steadiness of His hand. The beautiful is the face of God drawing our weary earth-stained eyes away from our selfish preoccupation. But art is not the stillness of form in the pose of death; over all true art and over every timeless form yet broods the eternal spirit, and our hearts in His presence are touched with the depths of the mystery of life.

The strange stillness of great art glows with a movement that transcends time as mere repetition or measurable succession. It is the movement of God in the midst of time, of His sovereign eternity fulfilling it. It is a symbol that signifies existence beyond our earthly scope. It is a hint of heaven. The beautiful escapes our ordinary categories of the good; it flies up over all moralisms. Art can only rest in the beautiful; yet the beautiful is no isolated frozen form quite eluding life. Our life must be for art's sake as well as art for our lives' sake, but the whole realm of the beautiful finds its meaning and power in the creative good that rises through every level of creativity up to the eternal life of the creating God. The beautiful is the still overflowing of the harmony of God's eternity spilling over into our confused self-seeking. The whole subject of human creativity and the beautiful, so seldom successfully combined, should be carefully studied by someone, in the light of the superspective of God's Agape.

What, for instance, is the relation between such still art as sculpture, painting and architecture, and music or poetry with all their movement and rhythm? All great art has more than formal harmony. It has the movement of life; at its highest the movement of purpose, character, intention, or a personal being creative within the repetition of the reactions which constitute the forms of all experience. Why are the vegetables painted by any member of the Dutch school, for instance, less great than a figure by Heraclitus, a frieze by Phidias, a mural by Michelangelo, a "Last Supper" by da Vinci, a "Crucifixion" by Grünewald, an altar scene by the Van Eycks, a face of an old Jew by Rembrandt, a "Prodigal Son" and even a "Thinker" by Rodin? Simply because these portray the higher level of creative character and life which both are and signify that tide too deep for sound or foam.

Consider the history of art. Here some reduce excellence to balance, perspective, the nude, tactile values, pattern, color, etc. But these are only, after all, the surface criteria. Art is great when it catches the depths of life in the realms of the greatest significance and focuses attention on some truth hidden in the obvious and the commonplace. And life is always existential harmony and motion—even a harbor by Turner with all its foggy loveliness must make us enter the experience of being there.

Great art calls for empathy rather than sympathy. It calls for participation through identification, for complete self-forgetfulness. The communion through art at its deepest has entered the stage of union where fellowship is beyond all self-consciousness, where individuality is not merged but fulfilled in membership. And such personal participation always has an undercurrent of motion, but motion in harmony. If art portrays depth of conflict, for instance, it fails of greatness unless over the whole there is the anticipated attainment of solution; even the peace of tragedy is greater than the avoidance of real life or mere unsolved problems. Art thus shares with religion the synthesis of the timeless. Or art fills time with the content which alone can make us want time "to stop," that is, really to keep existing in its present form. Art is not future purposes as much as self-perpetuation, repetition of judgment. This is the experience of "the heavenly places."

Yet all human art fails to find the full measure not only because it must deal with only a hint of heaven in terms of the scars of earthly existence, but because it must always deal with partial forms and limited motion. God and the fellowship as experienced, living realities alone offer the heart its final haven. That is why human love wants time to stop at its highest, the best it knows; yet human love, too, is a pale image of God's broken and distorted Agape on the grumbly waves of life's restless sea. Thus true art embodies the deeper motion of God's life, however minimally, along with the harmony of our approach to perfect form, the formal image of perfect purpose.

Whitehead is right that the energy of physics and of life are the same, explainable only from the reality of the latter. Thus music can be reduced almost crassly to mathematics, to harmony and counterpoint. The unbending forms of regulated relations are built on the material substrate of length and tenseness of string or size of opening, kind of material, intensity of force, etc. Yet great music is more than movement and formal harmony. Great music rises up into the heart of life. Beethoven's *Pastoral Symphony* has the pleasing undertone of thunderstorms and folk music; but Brahms rises to the intellectual appeal of the pleasures of thought; while Bach's "Come Sweet Death" and his great Masses speak of the endless mystery and assurance of human life in the light of God. It is useless to separate art from life. Supercilious critics and sophisticated devotees of it, who live in part-response, starved souls living on what is great and good yet deeply dying from lack of the one thing needful, do separate the two. But form of harmony, in whatever degree of form of flux and form in flux, is an abstraction. It has validity but no adequacy.

Great music speaks not only great thoughts, but the language of great being. The content of music, whether consciously understood or merely implicit in both artist and listener, is like to the content of painting or sculpture in comparison to the measurements of an abstract man or a general scene. Perhaps the response to music and to any great art is so much a whole-response of emotion, mind, and even the deeper will below conscious and particularized decision, that all specific or concrete thoughts are swallowed up in the symphony of the total meaning. To reduce great art to particularized meanings is to sin against it. Even a particular scene like the "Descent from the Cross" or a specific oratorio like *The Creation* must point beyond the historical instance to the eternal within it, the reality that causes history to arise; but such eternity, when Agape is understood as ultimate, as the content of Eternal Spirit, is never cold, abstract, formal. It is the full synthesis of form and content, of flux and form, of character and freedom, of stability and creativity.

We hear a great deal from certain modern poets that a poem, for instance, must signify nothing. It simply exists. It just is. This either means atomism in whole-response, or else some Platonic realm of self-existent values. Both are philosophically inadequate concepts. Yet to say that a poem merely means, simply signifies, is to land in the impossible reduction of everything to relations, without any adequate degree of self-being, landing us either in some contradictory universal relativism or in some absolute which swallows up the relations, thus again reducing history to unreality and destroying thereby the ground of all dependable knowledge.

Obviously a poem is a historic novelty, but not a sheer miracle. When Tennyson called Milton a "mighty-mouth'd inventor of harmonies," he spoke a half-truth. *Paradise Lost* was not written from all eternity. That is a historic creation. But it is also an arrangement of ideas and language not invented by Milton, obviously, and those in turn are historical occurrences referable to the nature of the existential ultimate, combining freedom and necessity, past and future, possibility and actuality, creative creatures with conditions of creation. A great poem simply is itself, of course, but by being itself it also signifies far beyond itself in proportion to its greatness.

The same is true of all great literature. It is common to dignify our low level of novels, for instance, by the need of keeping art for art's sake. We are asked to keep the question of morals out of literature. Conventionality, primness, and respectability based on fear of false taboos are one thing. Great basic morality, nevertheless, is another thing. And no plot and no character can be great that does not offer genuine human depths of problems and also genuine degrees of solution. Aristotle's theory of art as vicarious experience and solution is thus far well founded.

Great literature finds some level of transcendence, some hint of heaven, some power beyond the ordinary approaches and common defeats of life. But the plot must be conceived greatly and deftly executed. *The Rise of Silas Lapham*, for instance, lacks something of the convincing quality of Storm's *Immensee*. Both teach important lessons of life, but the latter more subtly. Moralism and morality must be distinguished. Greater than morality, moreover, is the spiritual category of being. Being is ever greater than doing or having. Such being defies the smug categories of mere conventionality, but such defiance is surely by itself not greatness. Greatness is ever positive solution within permanence of perspective. There is, therefore, real need to work out the meaning of art in terms of truth—God as Agape.

10. Two more points we want to single out as crucial. Agape is fellowship-making, breaking down barriers and creating all things ever new. When we are in the Holy Spirit we know that the deepest meaning of our being here, our past and our future, is the creation of the family of God. Agape is, as Augustine says, God's love for everyone as if He cared for him alone "and so for all as if they were but one."[48] It is God alone creating fellowship

[48] Augustine, "Confessions," *The Nicene and Post-Nicene Fathers*, Vol. I, p. 67.

through His Holy Spirit wherein alone lie reality and rest. It is complete concern for every member of the fellowship, including self, according to God's purpose for him within the fellowship, where to live is to live no longer in isolation and over against others but in suffering and sacrifice with and for others or in creative joy and co-operation, under and with God, with and for others.

Agape is the serving of others and the working for and with them because God Himself serves in utter humility each and all and works ever completely for and with each and all. Agape is the finding of all our securities and satisfactions within the fellowship of God's love as revealed in His Son. Agape is the freedom and faithfulness in fellowship as both light and life which give life its final and fullest zest and meaning. Agape is fellowship fulfillment through self-giving. Agape is the losing of the isolated self, self-enclosed and shut out, by the finding of the essential self that lives only within the Christian fellowship, God's full fellowship for all who see it—except for those who shut themselves out, while they do see.

Two basic questions of life are how to be saved and how to serve. In Agape they go together. Agape is the eucharistic fellowship of eternal praise to God by the servants that shall both serve Him and yet also reign with Him for ever and ever. Agape is the everlasting fellowship of the saved. Agape is endless life. It is the fellowship of His suffering and the power of His resurrection. Agape is the fellowship that knows neither end nor limits to the abundance of its life.

11. Most important of all, as we have stressed throughout, Agape is defined as Jesus Christ. He is our selective actual, history's most high, the fulfiller not only of the law but of reason, our truest index of ultimate reality, the peak point of process. He is the creative emergence which as the historic exception where Agape first became central in life and thought made it known as central in cosmos and conduct, and thus made Agape the exemplification of our essential being, of our potential destiny.

He. is the concrete individual who can best serve as our cosmic universal. He is living truth, actualized history. He is the person who best serves as a cosmic principle. He is the purpose who most fully illuminates the nature of the whole process. He is the height that is fully related to the long and deep mountain slopes below.

Agape gets its meaning dominantly from him. He is the judge of all as the Word becomes flesh. His own flesh, earthly life, is itself judged by the consistency of that union as meaning and action which is Agape. The weaknesses of the flesh are judged by the fullness of the Spirit.

He is the savior of all only as he mediates eternal Agape. He could of himself do nothing, he knew, but the Father worked in him. He is the door that opens, not that shuts out. Through him we see God's way with all that never have or can know of his historic work. God alone is our Savior, our final personal Savior, in His time and His way. But this God, this Agape, was truly and determiningly, conclusively in Christ.

This conclusive revelation is of the living God, of a Thou, of a relationship which can be had only through reaction, when He is made the center of our lives, the most important and the most real. Jesus is our existential ultimate, or the content of history and experience, which most conclusively indicates what is ultimately most important and most real, most true and most right. He is the decisive instance in history for or against whom we must decide. Without this decision, this ultimate decision, this absolute decision, he cannot be truly known from within and confirmed by experience to be the Son of God. He is the way but we cannot know it until we walk in it. The bridge is down between God and us, the bridge that spans the full distance between us, but we cannot get across except we use it. Yet it is there for all to see.

Truth in the ultimate sense must be personal, combining most fully action and meaning, the particular with the universal. Here is no secondary philosophical system. Here is a life that is our light, a person who is our truth. Nor is it a human and historical person who is central. It is God's personal Word out of eternity. It is God Himself, the divine Agape which took on flesh in a decisive manner for all times. Unless this be true we have no mediator, nor full salvation. God is the central actor in coming, in sending, in revealing, in healing, in suffering, in rising again. We must be weak with Jesus that we might live with him *through the power of God.* God was in Christ reconciling the world unto Himself.

"He who comes 'of the flesh' comes also of the direct action of God. The Consummator is also an Invader. He is the final bursting through of the divine into the stream of history."[49] "For how many so ever be the promises of God in him is yea. Wherefore also through him is the Amen, unto the glory of God through us."[50] He gave us "the light of the knowledge of the glory of God in the face of Jesus Christ."[51] "We cannot conceive the Living God; we can only perceive Him in His word."[52] "God in Christ—this is a sinner's only religion."[53] "The Christian apprehends God not merely in what He *is,* but also in what He *does*—that is, he apprehends God as the immediate agent in certain events, pre-eminently in that series of events which constitute the coming of our Lord. God *sent* His Son; God *came* in Christ; God *took* our nature—such phrases as these are integral to the expression of the Christian faith."[54]

Our insistence on God's action through a concrete person is altogether necessary, for our existential ultimate must be through some historic content, as we have seen, and only the personal will do. We insist on him not to narrow the Way artificially. The meat of the matter is obstacle enough to the natural man, that he

[49] Lewis, *The Philosophy of the Christian Revelation,* p. 48.
[50] II Corinthians 1:20.
[51] II Corinthians 4:6.
[52] Brunner, *Man in Revolt,* p. 103.
[53] Mackintosh, *Types of Modern Theology,* p. 145.
[54] Micklem, *What Is the Faith?* p. 55.

must die to self if he is truly to live, that he must die in full surrender to God in order to be raised up by Him into fullness of life; to become a new creature, a life within a new center; to find a new source of drive, a new perspective. We insist, rather, when we insist on the selective actual as our most adequate basis of truth, on the personal nature of God as the fullest truth we can find, as the most truthful dynamic synthesis of faith and reason.

We do not want, by any means, to minimize the nature of process; we do not want to belittle principles of explanation; we want only to emphasize concretely according to the nature of truth that all processes and principles in the end go back for their final meaning and function to the Person whom Jesus called Father and who wrought through Jesus the incoming of a new age, the final age, the age of the Kingdom, where all things become the means and media of the fellowship which He creates and all lives are to be explained, judged, and saved in the light and the power of God as Agape.

The life of Jesus, being history's most high, is not essentially explainable in terms of past history. It is essentially a miracle. It is essentially a mystery. *As Agape central in cosmos and conduct it is a discontinuity.* For this reason symbols are often more suggestive than explicit interpretations. To be true they must express real facts, yet facts which signify more than they say because they are beyond our ordinary category of explanation. They are both exceptional and exemplary, combining discontinuity with continuity, mystery with meaning. Thus symbolic are, for instance, the Virgin Birth and the Atonement and the Resurrection. Their truth is not that of biology, sociology, or simple history. Their truth consists in the imposition and superposition *on* these levels of continuity facts *in history* which primarily express a new order of being, a new level of life, a new kind of operation, a new age of reality.

Whenever this true superdimension which is the determinative reality is lost, so are the power and the truth of the Gospel. Our explanations and inquiries must be in this light, the light of the reflexive superspective. In the deepest and fullest sense of the word our ultimate perspective is supernatural.

The main part of this book reveals how our principle of explanation illuminates with a new and fuller light the whole problem of evil. The treatment of each succeeding topic will both illustrate the adequacy of our analysis and test it. In the end truth must be self-confirming in our deepest thinking and living. In an even fuller way than Hartshorne meant it, we shall surely find that "the divine as love is the only theme adequate to the cosmic symphony."[55]

[55] Hartshorne, *Man's Vision of God*, p. 216.

Faith and Reason

The leading line of *Faith and Reason* was that only what is most high within process can adequately be called most real. Truth, we found, *must by the very nature of knowledge be a living synthesis in thought and deed of knowledge and faith.* Truth cannot, that is, on the one hand, be based merely on what is here and now actual, for the evidence of just that actual points beyond itself to its own fulfillment. The most basic fact about rational knowledge is, in truth, that process points beyond itself. Process points ahead—in line with its highest attainment or most significant arrival. Nor can truth, on the other hand, simply be equated outright with faith, both because the content of adequate faith which is the most high in history must be selected by the best knowledge possible, thus making our knowledge of truth available only through our knowledge of our historic process, and also because, oppositely, the end indicated by process is obviously in our day far from fulfilled, thus leaving a gap for faith which cannot by our very situation be secured by reason, a chasm of unverifiable becoming, of sheer believing, between truth and faith.

This gap between eternity and time cannot possibly be *filled* by either faith or knowledge. It can only be pointed to by reason and bridged by faith. It can be filled only by actual events, by the concrete fulfillment of Purpose by process, by the historic realization of the eternal Intention. We were consequently left in *Faith and Reason* with the conclusion that all of us inescapably live primarily by faith. The only question is this: By what kind of faith?

The only adequate faith is found in the most high. There faith and knowledge are both at their best. There faith is at the same time supported by knowledge as fully as possibly can be, while it must nevertheless also remain unproved by such knowledge. To live in truth as far as one can is thus to keep deciding from within our best knowledge far beyond our best knowledge where the content of faith at the same time both fulfills and yet also denies the best that we can know.[1]

We tend to live in either a false both-and or a false either-or. We live in a false both-and when we view all things from our faith in the highest in a smooth speculative mood. Then faith simply fulfills and *transcends* reason. There is then no recognition that rational knowledge isolated from the faith it implies but cannot require actually contradicts the full perspective of faith. Such both-and thinking refuses to acknowledge the necessary element of human decision, which resolves the tension by a partly unwarranted "anticipated" attainment, the element of paradox which exists between time and eternity, or process and Purpose. From the point of view of our strictest thinking based on our partial evidence, there is an arbitrary, even if not absurd, element in faith.

On the other hand, when we give full sway to an either-or position we fail to see or we forget that reason points to faith, process to Purpose, history to Eternity. We do not observe, moreover, that all must live *by some faith primarily* and that all other faiths are more arbitrary and absurd *exactly to reason*. An all-and position preserves the unity both of reason and of faith and is legitimate in the explanatory perspective. An either-or position does justice to the contradictions between reason and faith when both are

[1] Cf. *Faith and Reason*, Chapters 3, 4.

made into self-sufficient ultimate standards. This either-or element is legitimate in the existential perspective.

Faith and reason both complement and contradict each other. Only a dynamic synthesis will do. This dynamic synthesis is the adequate content of right whole-response and in the end not only includes but transcends whole reason. Faith and reason as human interpretations and responses are flooded over their banks by revelation. This revelation is more than the coming of the new into historic process whereby knowledge and faith both grow. It is also the summation of insight and of intimate fellowship relations between our small *i*'s and God's great Thou. It is the making real and vibrant to the finite spirit his Ground and Goal, the Eternal Creator Spirit, our Father and our God.

The historic content of right religion, the pivot of faith, must not only be selected in terms of the right knowledge of our process as a whole, but also be assessed and certified in relation to it. In order legitimately to form the content of adequate faith, history's most high must consequently be truly and fully representative of the truest meaning, best worth, and most basic reality of process. It must be actual, a concrete instance of human history and of human experience, a down-to-earth, bedrock reality, not merely a theory unconfirmed in human experience and history.

This selective actual,[2] however, truly to constitute the most high must also be selectively ideal,[3] that is, it must offer at the same time (1) the fullest capacity for explaining, in the sphere of knowledge, the origins of process,[4] (2) the most adequate explanation of the whys and wherefores of evil, integrally and organically in relation to both the being and the meaning of process as incident to a fully satisfactory and adequate end, and (3) plenary power savingly and creatively to transform our present process by both providing the needed truth and generating the motiva-

[2] Cf. *ibid.*, p. 148.
[3] Cf. *ibid.*, p. 145.
[4] Cf. *ibid.*, pp. 159 ff.

tion to effect it. The most high of history must consequently be self-verifying[5] in the sense that the living in its light and power gives increasingly authentic security and satisfaction for living and developing, both to man as an individual and to society as a whole; while any other meaning and manner of living leads to inner frustration and, in the long run, to outward failure.

The most high is thus to be discovered by being selected existentially out of a dynamic synthesis of faith and reason. What is thus a continual process of selection, necessarily and by all, is the content of faith which constitutes the criterion of what is most high ultimately and ultimately most real. Such a process of selection becomes neither an arbitrary decision based on will or emotions primarily, nor a mere bit of theoretical investigation. It is ever an event which at its highest mingles completely life and thought, risk and seeing, hoping and having. Such a process, moreover, affords a superspective light, a light selected from within process yet in its full truth and reality pointing indescribably beyond process, a light which becomes in its fullness the judge, savior, and guide of what is now generally and actually true.

[5] Cf. *ibid.*, p. 152.

Index

Abraham, 113
Agape, 3, 19, 25, 45, 52, 71, 79, 131, 139 ff.
Ahimsa, 54
Alcoran, 102
Allison, George, 120
Analects, 142
Animal pain, 54 f., 61 ff., 133
Anselm, 70
Aquinas, 148, 153
Aristotle, 80, 160
Art, 156 ff.
Athanasius, 118, 48 n.
Augustine, 53, 160

Bach, 158
Baillie, 152
Barth, 72, 119
Bavinck, 54
Beauty, 96, 156 ff.
Beethoven, 158
Berdyaev, 47, 55
Bhagavad-Gita, 101, 142
Bible, 34, 49, 113, 114, 115
Blanshard, 59
Brahms, 158
Brightman, x, 55
Bring, 50
Brunner, 143, 152, 155, 163

Calvin, 16

Calvinism, 50
Carlson, E., 50
Champion, 102 n., 142
Christ, 21, 32, 39, 45, 49, 57, 63, 102
Christian Scientist, 13
Church, 120
Cochrane, 152, 153
Colossians, 57, 77, 145
Compossible, 70, 72, 130, 131
Corinthians, I, 24, 68, 121, 136, 144, 153
Corinthians, II, 31, 34, 121, 144, 163
Cross, 21, 24, 25, 49, 51, 53, 57, 68, 73, 84, 129, 130

Darwin, 54
Deane, 70
Devil, 44, 50
Dhammapada, 142
Dickie, 153
Dostoievsky, 152
Drama, 17
Dualism, 3

Eckhardt, 50
Ends, 10, 68 ff., 130
Ephesians, 65, 78, 144
Evans, D., 54
Evolution, 62 ff., 109
Existential perspective, 123 ff., 128, 131, 137